Hidden Tuscany

Hidden Tuscany
Unusual Destinations and Secret Places

Massimo Listri
Cesare M. Cunaccia

RIZZOLI
NEW YORK

To Mary T. Wolfe, a Tuscan at heart
C.C.

Previous pages:
Page 2: Benozzo Gozzoli, La cavalcata dei Magi, *detail from the frescos in Palazzo Medici Riccardi in Florence.*
Pages 4 and 5: Garden at Uzzano.
Page 6: Landscape near Bargino (above); Tuscan countryside near Castellina in Chianti (below).
Page 7: View of Sorano (above); Countryside near Montefiridolfi (below).
Page 8: Castiglioncello.
Page 9: View from one of the towers of San Gimignano.

First published in the United States of America in 1999 by
RIZZOLI INTERNATIONAL PUBLICATIONS, INC.
300 Park Avenue South, New York, NY 10010
Reprinted in 2002

First published in 1999 by
RCS Libri S.p.A., Milan

ISBN 0-8478-2223-0
LC 99-74783

Translation: Judith Goodman
Graphic Design: Sottsass Associati/Mario Milizia, Paola Lambardi
Typesetting: LexiStudio/Tiziana Cester

Printed and bound in Italy

CONTENTS

INTRODUCTION

All over the world, the name of Tuscany conjures up images of great cities of art amid a hilly landscape picked out by cypress and olive trees, themselves the frequent subjects of the region's age-old pictorial heritage. The art of Tuscany is most identified with the extraordinary era of the Renaissance; yet just as the region's landscape is far more diverse than many realize, its cultural history reveals an impressive range of influences and artistic movements. It might well be most accurate to refer to Tuscany in the plural, so many worlds make up its cultural universe. There are so many keys needed to unlock the secret of the Tuscan spirit, the exeptional quality of its art—from the legacy of mercantilism embodied by the Medici to the interaction between Catholic faith and mystic practice that has long been characteristic of the region.

One remarkable aspect of this history is the Mannerist movement, which blossomed in the late Renaissance. It was forged in the tormented contrasting light and dark of the Florence of the late fifteenth century. In the secret grottos of the Mannerist garden, monsters and magic symbols, alchemy and necromancy play shadow games that surprise many art lovers who stumble across them. And these cultural arcana also find their place in the cities. Fantastic and disturbing creatures lurk above tympana and portals, come to life among the stuccos and graffiti of sixteenth-century facades. Mocking and scornful, they even crouch in the sacred penumbra of the Florentine churches. The superb villas of Tuscany also offer crucial insight into the region's artistic history: from the cultivated simplicity of the first Medici residences outside the walls of Florence, to the glowing, elaborate architecture of the Baroque.

Those who come to Tuscany with a taste for exploration will also discover a veritable galaxy of fascinating, little-known museums that add to the picture presented by the world-renowned institutions of the region. Many of these unusual museums are dedicated to the phantasmagoric, to scientific curiosities, to neglected and peculiar artistic trends. Any serious appreciation of the art and culture of Tuscany must also consider the period around the end of the nineteenth century, the fin de siècle characterized by avant-garde movements that drew their energy from the large colony of foreigners, particularly the English, that called the region home. During this period, the sleepy Tuscany of the Lorraine was invigorated by a tide of international cultural ferment. Yet always, dedication to the highest standards of craftsmanship remained the hallmark of Tuscan artistic endeavors. There is still so much to be disclosed, to be revealed to the interested traveler to this remarkable land. Tuscany remains—proud, inimitable, unique. Artistic treasures unparalleled are there for those who know how to uncover them among the folds of the complex, alluring reality that is Tuscany.

The exterior loggia of Villa Mansi at Lucca.

PLACES OF THE SPIRIT:
COUNTRY CHURCHES AND CATHEDRALS
OF THE ROMANESQUE AND RENAISSANCE ERAS

Detail of a Dominican monk from the frescos by Beato Angelico in the convent cells of San Marco in Florence.

The Tuscan spirit is a proud and argumentative one. The inhabitants of the region have often been accused of an excess of anticlericalism, of an anarchic, often outrageous propensity toward Reason at the expense of Spirit. Even the saints most revered in this land—St. Catherine of Sienna, for instance—have always played extraordinarily important civic and even political roles in society. Beyond this, mysticism has long played an undeniably significant role in Tuscan culture, even as the fundamental religious piety of the region is revealed in the Romanesque churches of the Valdarno and the Val d'Orcia. It can be seen in the legendary ruins of San Galgano, in the theological paintings of Beato Angelico, in the Arrezzo frescoes by Piero della Francesca.

By contrast, the great urban cathedrals of the region, erected during the era of the Comunes, reflect the pride of the *Civitas*, prioritizing Man above Divinity. This dualism, this dialectic, seems to resolve itself in the convent-like institutions of Tuscany, from Camaldoli to Vallombrosa, from the Badia Fiorentina to Monte Oliveto Maggiore, where worldly conflicts seem to disappear and lose their meaning, as the ways of the spirit take reassuring precedence.

Facing page: The unfinished green and white marble facade of the Badia in Fiesole.

THE FANTASTIC MEDIEVALISM
OF THE PIEVE DI GROPINA

The country church of San Pietro in Gropina, hidden in thick vegetation, far from the village, gives the impression of still being fully immersed in the Middle Ages. Time seems suspended in the vicinity of this holy building that seems to rise from nowhere.

The stone facade of the tower is massive and austere, and shows signs of many restorations. The first restoration probably took place in 1422, the date carved on the architrave of the portal. Almost in the center of the facade is the Medici coat of arms of Leo X beneath a small mullioned window. The name Gropina is apparently derived from the Etruscan word *Krupina*, meaning village or inhabited area. The oldest document in which Gropina is mentioned concerns a donation by Charlemagne to the abbey of Nonantola in 780. The church was erected around the year 1000, and it is flanked by a massive bell tower, dated 1233.

The interior is in the plan of a basilica, unadorned and dimly illuminated by the light that filters through the narrow openings. Three naves define the space, which is punctuated by powerful monolithic columns enriched by decorated capitals. A semicircular apse with a double row of columns marks the legacy of Roman architecture.

The space is adorned with elements from both Christian and pagan narrative, eagles clutching their prey in their talons, tigers and lions rampant, stylized flowers sculpted in stone, with texts from the Old and New Testaments serving as captions. In San Pietro, the wide-ranging imagination of Medieval Man comes to life. The church, though dominated of course by the sacral, is touched throughout by vestiges of the pagan, of ancestral cults, of superstition and magic. These elements cohere and speak to us directly, surprisingly immediate and comprehensible.

Among the decorations that grace the capitals are clusters of grapes, bunched in pairs along trios of superimposed, three-dimensional branches. On the lower parts of the pulpit, this decorative grape motif is repeated. The work has been performed with such virtuosity that it has the lightness of lace. The centerpiece is the round pulpit, which rests on two lateral pillars and a pair of entwined columns. Supporting the weight of the pulpit is a beautiful caryatid ensemble with five stocky figures, arms uplifted. The figures are remarkably expressive and intense. In the center an eagle holds an open book, beside a man and a lion—these represent the three evangelists John, Matthew, and Mark. The panels contain decorative geometrical forms of small circles superimposed one on top of the other, generating a visual effect similar to that of the rings that form around a pebble thrown into still water. On the left stands an angel with widespread wings. On the right, a man hangs upside down, devoured by two serpents.

From top to bottom: Capital with vine-shoots. Capital with two lions facing. A sculpted panel on the pulpit.

Facing page: Pulpit of the Pieve in Gropina.

THE MYSTIC GEOMETRY
OF SAN MINIATO

San Miniato dominates Florence and the surrounding hills, from Fiesole to Settignano. Standing atop Monte delle Croci, it is the most significant example of central Italian Romanesque architecture.

Long under the care of the Benedictines of Cluny, San Miniato passed into the hands of the Olivetan monks who in 1373 acquired the palazzo of the Florentine bishops that stands near the church. The foundational structure of the church, however, is much older still. It already existed in the time of Charlemagne, and was rebuilt by Bishop Hildebrand at the beginning of the eleventh century. The facade is of a later date, and in its composition is similar to the Baptistry of the Duomo in Florence. It is decorated in alternating white and green marble. On the lower of the facade's two levels, there are five arches with Corinthian pilasters. These arches lead to three real portals and two of marble with a *trompe l'oeil* effect. The second level of the facade is separated into three parts by grooved pilasters that divide the geometric decorations of the marble of the lateral spans from the central part in which there is a large window crowned by a classical tympanum. Above the opening there is a mosaic, probably dating from the beginning of the thirteenth century, representing Christ enthroned with Mary and St. Minias. Higher up, on the gable, decorated with little false arches, is the symbol of the guild of wool merchants, a powerful Florentine corporation that administered the church of San Miniato for much of the thirteenth century.

Details of mirrored marbles on the church walls.

The second level of the facade corresponds with the central nave of the church, according to the original eleventh-century structure, recalling the style of Lombardian churches. The median space is separated by the lateral naves by a series of columns, some decorated in the style of restored Roman capitals. The high altar is raised above the central nave and is overhung by a simple wooden beamed ceiling. The floor is covered with fine marble mosaics depicting lions, doves, and signs of the Zodiac. Given its prominent position, towering on a hilltop above Florence, and visible from every part of the city, the church has taken on a special importance in the Florentine imagination. From high above it dominates the activities of the medieval city center, the nineteenth-century avenues, and the disorderly and anonymous modern suburbs.

Facing page: Column sustaining the lectern of the pulpit, decorated with symbols of the Evangelists.
Following pages: Luminous interior of the church.

THE REFUGE OF THE WHITE MONKS
AT MONTE OLIVETO MAGGIORE

There is a certain metaphysical quality about the abbey of Monte Oliveto Maggiore and the site on which it stands. It was here in 1313 in the shadow of a protective grove of cypress and olive trees—the so-called "desert of Accona"—that Bernardo Giovanni Tolomei, a brilliant, aristocratic doctor at law, found the perfect place for his spiritual retreat from the world. The abbey was and remains a paradise of mystical elegance, where ethic and esthetic flow together in unrivaled harmony. With his friends Patrizio Patrizi and Ambrogio Piccolomini, Tolomei created a sanctuary between the exclusive walls of this refined *turris eburnea* where adherence to the rules of the Benedictine order could renew a sense of spiritual and intellectual integrity. Traces remain of this period of the monastery in the entrance's palazzo, constructed in 1393 and surmounted by a square tower with battlements and buttresses. Magnificent enamels of a Madonna in the style of the school of della Robbia shine above the gateway.

After the first phase of building in the fourteenth century, the complex was further developed during the Renaissance, until it was finished in 1526. Some restoration was carried out in the nineteenth century. Inside the sheltered universe of the abbey, the "white" alchemist monks alternated their experiments with meditation and prayer. They concocted their medicinal mixtures from the rare herbs that they cultivated in their precious garden, and created exquisitely illuminated manuscripts in gold. The splendid frescoes of Signorelli and Sodoma in the background of the abbey's vast cloister are a testimony to this quietly elegant way of life. The sublime austerity of Luca Signorelli's work, painted between 1497 and 1498, and covering the west wing of the cloister, is a play on alternating colors between the leitmotiv of the monks' tunics and the drab green, acid magenta, and liquid turquoise representing the laity. In 1508 Sodoma concluded the cycle that had been prematurely interrupted by Signorelli. Sodoma's work, recalling that of Leonardo, is in a sophisticated and fluid style, exemplified in the depiction of the luxurious, expensive garments of a noble gentleman. The work conbines an attention to detail characteristic of Northern Renaissance style with an airy, spacious quality typical of the Florentine and the Roman.

The rich intarsios of the choir of the monastery's church date from this same period. The building, elaborately decorated with exotic animals, birds, and images of the Sienese landscapes by Fra Giovanni da Verona, was completely transformed by Giovanni Antinori in the eighteenth century.

Two panels of the church choir with wood inlay by Fra Giovanni di Verona.

Facing page: The Great Cloister of Monte Oliveto Maggiore with Luca Signorelli's frescos.

THE TRIUMPH
OF MANNERISM

Andrea Del Sarto, details from the fresco
Caesar Receiving Tribute From Egypt, *1521.*
Villa Poggio a Caiano, Leo X Chamber.

Facing page: Agnolo Bronzino, Allegory
(from a drawing by Michelangelo).
Florence, Galleria degli Uffizi.

The Mannerist style was the outgrowth of a combination of new, unusual, and often tormented attitudes that challenged the harmonious conjunction of Christianity and neo-Platonism, the basis of the very idea of humanistic culture. The crucible of the synthesis of this artistic ideology was the Florentine circle of Andrea del Sarto, Mariotto Albertinelli, and Fra Bartlomeo. The artists who emerged from this school, which was active around 1510 to 1515, manifested a distinct vocation for cultural research, for an anguished mode of representation, and for sophisticated experimenting. They are characterized by a devouring spirit of restlessness, by a saturnine melancholy of the soul. The Italian political crises of the age troubled the conscience of these men, who were affected as well by the religious debate generated by the Reformation and following that, the Catholic Counter-Reformation. Theirs was also an age that was shocked out of its security by the discoveries that expanded the once-unquestioned geographical boundaries of the known world. These were caught in and captivated by an irreconcilable dualism, suspended between a fascination with magic, the necromantic arts, the irrational and the new frontier of scientific knowledge and the conception of the universe itself, as reconfigured by the Copernican revolution. In the Mannerist style, everything is permeated with doubt, with uncertainty. Images and ideas both are confusing, complicated. The products of Mannerism constitute the tangible testimony of an age in crisis.

The first phase of Mannerism is predominated by experimentation. The visual approach is strident and excessive. It tends to the grotesque, and presents itself as a subversion of the classical canon. It veers wildly and freely from orthodox artistic convention. It is inspired by the darkest considerations, by the unusual implications of the great artists of the Renaissance, from Leonardo to Michelangelo. At the same time it has clearly been influenced by northern Flemish and German artists, from Albrecht Dürer to Lucas van Leyden. This early Mannerist era was the age of Rosso Fiorentino and Pontormo in Florence and of the extraordinary example of Beccafumi in Siena. It was a time of great creativity, of artistic innovations still remarkable for their idiosyncrasy and originality.

*Rosso Fiorentino, detail from the
Deposizione dalla Croce, 1521.
Volterra, Pinacoteca of the Comune.*

By the mid-sixteenth century the pursuit of research for its own sake, the continuous and insistent questioning, the taste for dissonance, even for the changing sociopolitical conditions and for the Counter Reformation's call to order, had all abated. In this second phase of Mannerism, that of the *Bella Maniera*, Giorgio Vasari, from Arezzo, dominated the artistic scene. Inspired by his own legendary self-admiration and the opulence of the courtly life of which he relentlessly partook, he celebrated his success by building a residence which, he was rightly convinced, would be famous forever. Agnolo Bronzino could be considered the connecting link between the two very different and successive moments of the *Maniera*. In his youth he was a pupil of Pontormo and then the official portraitist at the Medici court of Cosimo I. His splendidly cold and elegant dynastic icons still have the feeling of restlessness or dissatisfaction, the inner rage and melancholy transmitted by his teacher.

Particularly in its most esoteric aspects, its interest in sorcery, for instance, Mannerism held great appeal for the Surrealist artists of our own century. Moreover, as we near the end of the millennium during a period in which the irrational and ancestral fears of humanity seem to have discovered new and fertile ground, Mannerism speaks powerfully to this historical moment as well. The products of Mannerism and the lives of its artists reflect a very familiar anxiety, a desire for definite answers, for reassurance, for spiritual peace.

*Facing page:
Agnolo Bronzino, Portrait of Eleonora di Toledo.
Florence, Galleria degli Uffizi.*

IN THE FOOTSTEPS
OF PONTORMO AND ROSSO

Rosso and Pontormo were two of the most significant painters of the early Mannerist era. Devoured, each in his way, by profound intellectual and emotional disturbances, their lives as well as their art are representative of that era's spirit. Jacopo Carucci da Pontormo and Giovanni Battista di Jacopo, known as Rosso Fiorentino, were both born in 1494, both sons of artists. Direct testimony of their parallel lives is handed down to us, as usual, by way of Vasari who knew them well. Rosso, a physically attractive man, was a wanderer, a musician and a philosopher with a propensity for quarrel, and for violent, heated dialectic controversies. Pontormo, by contrast, was possessed by a more meditative spirit, and his entire career took place in the vicinity of Florence. Although they had different temperaments, there seems to have been a deep bond that united them. They began their artistic careers working together as pupils and collaborators of Andrea del Sarto at the Santissima Annunziata in Florence. Even as they continued with their maestro, between 1513 and 1516 they worked on the *Chiostro dei Voti* in the same church as artists in their own right. Pontormo painted the fresco of the *Visitation*, Rosso that of the *Assunta*. After the brief and chaotic reign of Savonarolo in Florence, the city could no longer be that radiant center of cultural rebirth that it had been in the time of Lorenzo the Magnificent. Still, reformist ideas were circulating, and new fonts of artistic inspiration, like the Flemish prints and those of Dürer, could hardly leave two curious and sensitive talents like Rosso and Pontormo unaffected.

In 1518, the *Pala di Santa Maria Nuova*, by Rosso, was summarily rejected by its patron, while Pontormo had his first success with the animated composition entitled *Pala Pucci*, in the Church of San Michele Visdomini. In 1521 Rosso produced his masterpiece in the town of Volterra. The extraordinary *Deposizione dalla Croce* is now in the Pinacoteca of the Comune, but it was originally hung in the chapel of the Croce di Giorno, annexed to the church of San Francesco. In its provocation, the painting is a virtual manifesto for Mannerism. The vertical composition is contradicted by the scale and the gestures of the characters. The colors are radiant and full-blooded. The main impression is anti-classical, with echoes of Sienese Gothic and traces of Flemish influence side by side with the humanistic lessons of Masaccio and Piero della Francesca. There is a cold and watchful character to the painting, in the silent and at the same time eloquent pain of the figures, in the spasmodic gestures of the anatomical

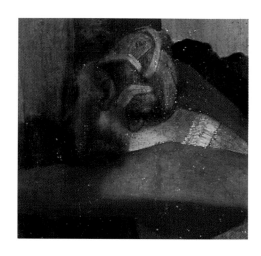

Above and facing page: Rosso Fiorentino, details from the Deposizione dalla Croce, *1521. Volterra, Pinacoteca of the Comune.*

forms, facial details, excessively luxuriant clothing. He also painted the *Pala di Villamagna* in Volterra for a country church near the town. It is in the Museo Diocesano d'Arte Sacra. In 1523 the altar piece containing the *Sposalizio della Vergine* finally confirmed Rosso's fame in the eyes of the Florentines. The piece is notable for its colors that blur towards the bottom and the way in which its structure is resolved in two tangential elipses in the form of the officiating priest. It was created for the altar of the Chapel of Giuseppe and Maria in San Lorenzo, the most typical of the Medici churches, and it still can be seen there. In 1524 Rosso was in Rome among the Florentine artists who hoped to be favored by Cardinal Giulio de' Medici who had just been elevated to the papacy as Pope Clement VII. He left only two frescoes that were commissioned of him by the Cesi family for their own chapel in Santa Maria della Pace, but established a firm friendship with the patron Leonardo Tornabuoni, a papal counsellor and a Florentine like Rosso himself.

The diaspora of artists that followed the Imperial sack of Rome in 1527 took Rosso to Perugia and then to Borgo San Sepolcro, where Lorenzo Tornabuoni was bishop. At this point Rosso's commissions were strictly religious as he had not followed up on the private, patrician and urban patronage of the Cesi, the Ginori, and the Dei, for whom he had painted the altar piece of the same name and which can be seen at the Pitti palace. At Sansepolcro (as Borgo San Sepolcro is known today) Rosso was once more imbroiled in a quarrel. Embittered by the public sensation caused by the dispute, on Holy Thursday of 1530 Rosso departed for Pesaro and then went to Venice, where he was a guest of Pietro Aretino. He then set off for France, where he took part in the creation of a French version of the Mannerist style and where he died in 1540. A significant group of his works can be found at the Uffizi, where the *Pala di Santa Maria Nuova* is also held. Apart from the famous canvas with the cherub plucking a lute and the *Portrait of a Young Woman*, there is the painting entitled *Moses Defends the Daughters of Jethro*, probably finished in 1523. It stands out in its sculptural power and in its paradoxically abstract anatomical quality.

Pontormo, as noted earlier, stayed close to Florence for the entire course of his career. As a young artist he was a frequent visitor to the workshops of Piero di Cosimo and Leonardo. In 1515, on the occasion of the arrival in Florence of Pope Leo X de' Medici, he painted the *Veronica* fresco in the Papal Chapel in Santa Maria Novella. In its accentuated gestures and the monumentality of the figure, it recalls the work of Michelangelo. Between 1519 and 1521 he painted the fresco *Vertumno e Pomona* for the Medici villa at Poggio a Caiano. The plague in Florence in 1523 forced him to take refuge at the Certosa del Galluzzo, three miles south of the city. Here he spent two years painting the lunettes in the great cloister with the *Storie della Passione*. The contrast with the peaceful *Arcadia* of Poggio a Caiano could not have been greater or more dramatic. Pontormo was inspired by Dürer's wood engravings, and stayed at the monastery long after he had completed his work there. Caught up in the Reformist tide then sweeping through the Catholic church, he became lost in theological speculation for a time. In 1525 he painted *Cena di Ammaus* for the guestrooms of the monastery. It is now in the Uffizi. Although one can see the influence of Dürer, it also signals a new and personal pictorial energy. Other admirable works by Pontormo are also on display at the Uffizi. Among these are the modelled *Portrait of Cosimo il Vecchio*, the splended *Dama col cestello di fusi*, the *Madonna col Bambino e San Giovannino*, also known as *La Carità*, and *La Madonna col Bambino e Santi*, where the collaborative effort of his pupil Bronzino can be observed. *The Adoration of the Magi* can be admired at the Pitti, as can the canvas entitled *Gli undicimila martiri*, dating to the end of the 1520s, a prelude to an extremely anguished pictorial phase in the life of the artist.

It is, however, the church of Santa Felicita, not far from the Ponte Vecchio in the direction of the Pitti Palace, that has the greatest number of works by Pontormo. He was entrusted with the decoration of the chapel bought in 1525 by Lodovico Capponi, a patrician Florentine banker. Pontormo, with the assistance of Bronzino, threw himself into the work with maniacal secrecy. Not even his patron was allowed to observe the work in progress. The fresco decoration of the chapel includes *The Annunciation* and the four *tondi* in the ceiling contain *Gli evangelisti*, which are partly ascribable to Bronzino. But the fulcrum of the artistic whole is without doubt the great canvas, *Il trasporto di Cristo al Sepolcro*, on the altar of the chapel.

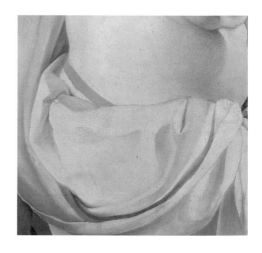

Above and facing page: Pontormo, details from
Il trasporto di Cristo al sepolcro.
Florence, Church of Santa Felicita.

The composition is of two groups at right angles to each other, one of the pious women, the other the figures carrying the body of Christ. The bloodless figure of Christ bowing forward in veneration is the counterpart of the Madonna who seems to be falling backwards. Mother and Son become centrifugal elements along the geometric axis traced between the shadowy female figure above and the figure crouched below in the foreground. Their searching hands emphasize the sense of fracture, piercing separation, farewell. The range of colors employed, diaphanously clear and brilliant at the same time, bear no trace of chiaroscuro, no dense shadows. A metaphorical play of color and shadow that falls upon the naked skin of some of the figures superimposes itself like the female characters that are swallowed up by the sky. The radiant acid green above the Madonna creates a powerful tension with the golden yellow of the drapery that cloaks the crouched figure in the painting foreground.

The poetic *Visitazione*, a treatment of the theological mystery of the Incarnation, was painted around 1530 for the Pieve di Carmignano, in the Empoli region.

The suggestive division and symmetry of the two figures, the two silent spectators lost in contemplation of the void, the forewarning of drama, the eloquent meeting of glances full of meaning, fear, reassurance, the unnatural swelling of the clothes, transport the viewer into a realm of existentialist questions, of the arcane. For the Venice Biennale of 1995, American artist Bill Viola created a video installation of extraordinary emotional power inspired directly by the work of Pontormo.

Pontormo's last tormented undertaking, the *Giudizio* for the choir of the Laurentian basilica, was a complex of frescoes that were destroyed during the restoration of 1742, leaving possible only a reconstruction through the preparatory drawings.

From what we can see and imagine of it, this final work provided ultimate confirmation of the opinion of Vasari that Pontormo's "bizarre and fantastic brain never rested content with anything."

Pontormo, detail from Il trasporto di Cristo al sepolcro.
Florence, Church of Santa Felicita.

GIORGIO VASARI'S HOUSE OF FAME

Above: House of Vasari, detail of fireplace.

Below: Giorgio Vasari. Detail from Portrait
of Alessandro de' Medici.

Florence, Galleria degli Uffizi.

Vasari's flood of artistic and architectural production is made manifest in the
stupendous dynastic and allegorical celebration of the frescoes in Palazzo Vecchio in
Florence and in the autobiographical exaltation of his two residences, in Florence and
Arezzo. In works sacred and profane, Giorgio Vasari's extremely controlled technique,
his virtuoso eclecticism, his mastery of narrative and rhetoric, all give life to a "grand
manner" of opulence and ease. A touch of the bizarre and the self-consciously
extravagant are worked into the courtly flow of his pictorial narrative. The restless
quality so characteristic of the first phase of Mannerism is exorcised; now exquisitely
decorative elements, in elegant caprice, form a refined thread of allusions and
references that could only be deciphered by an exclusive, aristocratic group of initiates.

Vasari's house in Arezzo, the city of his birth, exemplifies this style and spirit. It was
a refuge for an artist who lived a vagabond life between the exhausting round of social
engagements to which he was obligated, and his prodigious artistic activity. Giorgio
bought the building in 1541 when he was still a young man. It was situated in the
Borgo di San Vito, and still under construction. When the work was completed, Vasari
decorated the four rooms on the first floor with frescoes inspired by his role as a court
artist and intended for a glorification both personal and vocational.

Not by chance in the first room, dedicated to "Fame and the Arts," the allegorical figure
of Fame proclaims the universal glory of the artist. She is flanked by figures representing
Painting, Sculpture, and Poetry, as well as eight portraits of various painters. They bear
witness to the artistic tradition of Arezzo and to Vasari's two ideal masters, Michelangelo
and Andrea del Sarto. Leaving the *Corridoio di Cerere*, one enters the *Camera di Abramo*
where there is a Michelangelo-like figure of God on the ceiling, surrounded by Peace,
Harmony, Virtue and Modesty floating in the air and dispensing abundance. The
Camera di Apollo e delle Muse is dominated by an Apollo who is about to play a viola
d'amore and is surrounded by the Muses. Hidden among them is the portrait of
Niccolosa Bacci, the daughter of a wealthy local merchant, whom the artist married in
1550. The splendid *Camera del Camino* is the height of Vasari's collection of portraits.
A *Venus* in gesso by Ammanati stands over the great hearth. The room is graced by
a superb Venetian wooden ceiling that circles around an octagonal painting, *La Lotta
della Virtù contro la Fortuna e l'Invidia* (*The Struggle of Virtue against Fortune and Envy*).

The wall decorations are also allegorical. The Michelangelo-like figures of the Virtues are placed over the doors and windows, and punctuate the monochrome landscapes in tones of bronze. They represent six episodes from the lives of six painters of antiquity, from Apelles to Parrhasius, from Zeuxis to Protogenes. As Vasari himself wrote: "Stories of ancient painters wander under Saturn." The symbolic alternations refer to Vasari's double mastery as a painter and an art historian. On the walls there are also *trompe l'oeil* and allusions to the family name in the great vases that stand in the two openings in the walls.

Two great ideas are at play in this room: the fundamental concerns of humanism and a fascination with the stars. Here the artist examines their mutual influence on the human character and its humors. The whole decorative complex of Giorgio Vasari's house in Arezzo delineates a lexicon that describes itself, that recounts its origins and becomes a parallel with human life. Art to describe art. Home of the artist, of Art and Fame.

Giorgio Vasari. Portrait of Alessandro de' Medici. Florence, Galleria degli Uffizi.

Giorgio Vasari. The Sala del Camino *in the House of Fame in Arezzo.*

FRANCESCO, BIANCA, AND BERNARDO

Francesco I de' Medici, Bianca Cappello and Bernardo Buontalenti, were responsible for a host of ambitious artistic and architectural projects, a range of fantastic and grandiose creations.

The marriage in 1565 of Imperial Francesco to Joanna of Austria was unhappy from the very start, as witnessed by the bride's disastrous entrance into Florence, which was delayed by a week because of bad weather. Francesco was to discover love in the guise of a beautiful seventeen-year-old Venetian, Bianca, of the patrician Cappello family. She had been abducted to Florence where she was unwillingly married to her kidnapper, Pietro Buonaventura. A request was made for her extradition and a price of two thousand ducats was put on the head of her seducer. The young woman's audience with Francesco led to an official liaison and a consequent uproar among the European courts. The future Grand Duchess of the Hapsburgs was particularly outraged. The Serenissima and the Cappello family protested violently, and the diplomats resorted to poisonous whisperings. Fueling the scandal, Francesco included Bianca among the women of honor at the Pitti Palace, unconcerned by the resentment of his consort. He went so far as to install Bianca in a superb palazzo in Via Maggio, not far from his own residence. The building, still in existence, was erected by Bernardo Buontalenti between 1567 and 1570 over a previous, fifteenth-century structure. It is one of the few remaining examples of graffito decoration, prevalent in the second half of the sixteenth century. Buontalenti was an alchemist and versed in the occult and necromantic sciences, and like his Medici protector he amused himself with a repertory of winged *fauni*, diabolical monsters, and other figures. The inamorata's *arme parlante*, a traveling hat, appears proudly, almost mockingly, on the main door (a play on her family name and the adventurous circumstances of her arrival in Florence).

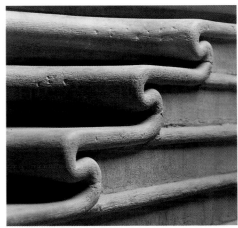

In 1576 Cosimo I died and Francesco became grand duke. Two years later Joanna of Austria's sad life came to an end at the age of thirty-one. There were now no obstacles between the two lovers, not even the insistent public gossip that Bianca was behind the series of fortunate deaths. Bianca tended to be fat and sickly and she was unable to give her consort the greatly desired heir to the Tuscan crown. The love story, however, did not seem to diminish. On October 12, 1579, the grand duke led a radiant Bianca to the altar. The Venetian Republic withdrew its condemnation and the Cappello family granted their pardon, and Bianca was pronounced a Real Daughter of San Marco. Still, the couple remained at the center of a hurricane of insults, under suspicion of conspiracies and witchcraft. They lived in relative modesty and near-seclusion. The grand duke loved the company of scholars and learned men like the cosmologist Ignazio Danti. He made

Details of the architectural decorations of Santa Maria Novella, Santo Stefano al Ponte, Poggio a Caiano.

Facing page: Facade of the palazzo of Bianca Cappello.

bronzes and repaired archeological finds with Cellini, but above all he loved the company of Buontalenti. With him Francesco had designed the fortress of Livorno, and invented weapons like the "devil's bomb," a kind of shrapnel device. He also enjoyed distilling essences and liqueurs, discovered a way to melt rock crystal, and managed to obtain the secret of porcelain, which until then had been kept by the Chinese. In the meantime, the city and its buildings were being covered with Medici busts, framed by elaborate scrolls. They were placed over portals and pediments, while the armes parlantes testifying to the new direction of the grand-ducal power appeared on the corners of public and private palazzos elaborately festooned with quartered crowns, papal tiaras, knightly orders, garlands, and masks. Dynastic symbols underwent the inevitable decorative transformation, contributing to an exaltation of metamorphosis, the real Mannerist canon.

The architectural code of that period was enriched with unusual shapes, often allusive and allegorical. In Florentine cultural circles the crisis of the naturalistic neo-Platonism of the early period of Humanism gave way to some disturbing organic-architectural combinations that sprang from Buontalenti's fertile imagination. Animal heads, grotesque masks, grimacing faces, natural and artificial shells, symmetric or capricious, spectral and diaphanous bats' wings, occult contortions of animal forms, monstrous membranes of pietra serena—all this contributed to the Mannerist effect of marvel and, in paradox, mirrored also the new interest in scientific discoveries. Even the classical caryatid underwent a metamorphosis, transformed in one case into an anthropomorphic stalk to hold up a holy water stoup. Similarly, the dialectic contamination between the converging flutes of a shell and the dynamic membrane of a bat's wing produced in 1574 the ray-like structure of a staircase by Buontalenti for the choir of Santa Trinità. The staircase is now in Santo Stefano al Ponte. In 1593 Buontalenti himself gave it a three-sided facade. These designs winked at the occult, even the satanic, with self-conscious irony. Spiral, redundant connections, coiled earlike shapes, reversed dados and pedestals, medallions, armorial bearings, extenuating twisted boundaries—all belong to the bizarre and mysterious language of Florentine Mannerism. The iconographic language of Mannerism was pregnant with arcane, occult references, applied literally in architecture and the decorative arts. Imaginative and sensational, works such as Buontalenti's staircase are a prelude to the development of the baroque.

From left to right and from above: Masks that decorate Florentine architecture in the age of Mannerism: in the courtyard of Palazzo Vecchio, in a private garden, at Santo Stefano al Ponte, in via dello Sperone, and in the grotto by Buontalenti at Boboli.

Facing page: Fountain attributed to Buontalenti in via dello Sperone in Florence.

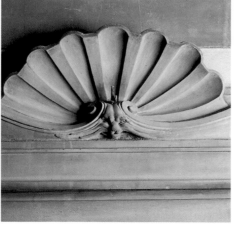

Above: Detail of the stairway at Santo Stefano al Ponte.

Below: Details of the decoration in Santa Maria Novella.

Above: Detail of the stairway in the Museo degli Argenti.
Below: Detail of the decoration in Santa Maria Novella
and detail of the stairway at Santo Stefano al Ponte.

THE MANNERIST GARDEN
AND ITS GROTTOS

The gardens of the palazzos and villas built in the second half of the sixteenth century were the ideal setting for a *mise-en-scène* of decorative jests and capricious theatrical experiments born of the typical Mannerist taste for deception. The architectural wings were made in the traditional manner, sometimes filled with greenery, and decorated with mobile contrivances and machines. Fanciful giants and robots might populate the scene, creating a continuous dialectical confrontation between art and nature.

The Mannerist garden was suffused with the same atmosphere of magic, of necromancy that also characterized the chambers of wonders or *wunderkammern* popular among the aristocracy of the time. These collections, intended to signify possession of the entire range of human knowledge and the owner's control over the natural universe, gathered together precious and fantastic objects composed of *naturalia*, *artificialia*, and *mirabilia*. Francesco I de' Medici's world-famous *studiolo* overflowed with rare and extravagant objects. Rudolf II of Hapsburg, owner of the most important of the *wunderkammern* of the late Mannerist age, was noted as well for his maniacal passion for alchemy. The private apartments of the sovereign contained collections of rock crystal, ostrich eggs or nautilus mounted in gold and silver, triumphs of exotic shells or portraits of strange and unusual beings. The parks of the houses and villas were filled with grottos, labyrinths, and fountains to match the same marvelous universe that was contained in the rooms inside. The garden of the Medici villa of Castello is the paradigm of sixteenth-century Italy's concept of the garden. Revealed here is the triumph of the Mannerist movement, the innovative and spectacular use of light and shade, expressed in theatrical inventions, surprising environments, and exotic and marvelous elements. The final geometry of the formal context, outlined by the box hedges, leads to the ideal form of a fountain standing in the center of a parterre. An opening in the terrace supporting the upper part of the garden leads to a hidden grotto enlivened by three fountains by Bartolomeo Ammannati. Around them is a group of suggestive animal sculptures in bronze, stone, and granite, made by sculptors of the circle of Giambologna. The exotic fauna blend naturally with the European and mythological. A lion is presented next to a goat, an ox near a fabulous unicorn. In another sculptured group a dromedary ridden by an ape stands out beside a stag. A boar and a leopard, an elk and a she-wolf, all are represented in a decorative context of artificial stalactites, twisted masks, incrustations of shells. Among the animals crowded into the left-hand

These pages: Sculptures representing animals in the grotto of the villa at Castello.

Above: Statues and monsters in the garden of the villa at Pratolino.

Facing page: The gigantic statue of the Appennino, work of Gianbologna.

niche is a bronze rhinoceros, an exotic animal *par excellence*, whose horn was greatly
prized for its presumed miracle-working and aphrodisiac properties. The three fountains
are in the form of sarcophagi. The central one is in red and black marble. The two on
either side, in light-colored marble, are decorated with garlands of fish, darting about
intertwining shells. The bronze birds, work of Giambologna, that decorated the ceiling
of the grotto are now kept in the Museo Nazionale of the Bargello.

Between 1568 and 1586 Bernardo Buontalenti built a great palace at Pratolino
for Francesco I and Bianca Cappello. It was completed under Ferdinando I, and the
residential building that resulted was sumptuous and rich in architectural inventions,
in the late Mannerist style. In the garden Bountalenti displayed a phantasmagoric
corpus of scenic inventions and play of water. There was an abundance of water in the
area, and it fed the park of Pratolino via an acqueduct that was five kilometers long.
Buontalenti's imagination was directed at both the amusement and the amazement
of the spectator. While the apparently bizarre play of water no longer exists, some
treasures that reflect the grandiose nature of the project remain: the gigantic statue
of *Appennino* by Giambologna, for instance, that hides a secret room in its head. In his
Voyage en Italie Michel de Montaigne described the construction of this new divinity
of the Mannerist pantheon: "they are building the body of a giant whose eyeball
is three cubits large." Baccio Bandinelli's *Giove* surveys the entrance to Pratolino,
a Medici Parnassus of incantations, a strange, precious, metaphorical garden of Armida.

Garden of Villa Demidoff at Pratolino.

*Facing page: Grottos and stretches of water in the
garden of Villa Demidoff at Pratolino.*
Following pages: The grotto at Pratolino.

With the passing of the years the villa was frequented less often by the descendants of the grand duke. It did, however, have a brief revival at the beginning of the eighteenth century when Prince Ferdinando retired there and staged a number of theatrical entertainments against the extraordinary backdrop of the villa. Buontalenti's construction was demolished in the Lorraine period and many of the marvels that had made the villa famous disappeared. The property then passed into the hands of the Russian Demidoff princes who owned it from the end of the nineteenth century until 1955.

Detail from a fountain in the garden at Boboli.

Our Mannerist journey, however, can end only in the Boboli gardens. They were designed by Tribolo in 1555 for Eleonora de Toledo, daughter of the viceroy of Naples and wife of Cosimo I, and completed under the supervision of Marco del Tasso. Vasari, once again, informs us how much the duchess loved grottos, and relates how she employed Baccio Bandinelli to build a "grotto full of the inhabitants of the submerged world and sponges frozen by water." But it was Bernardo Buontalenti between 1583 and 1593 who built the most spectacular and articulated grotto in the garden. It was an enchanted place, exemplifying the fantastic imagination of the Mannerists with its cornucopia of technical and symbolic equipment.

Beyond the portico altered by Vasari and the two sculptures by Bandinelli is the first room, which is the most brilliantly illuminated. Covering the walls are stuccos of human and animal forms, references to the myth of Deucalion and Phyrra escaping the flood. The frescos of the ceiling simulate a collapsed vault from which peer strange wild animals and satyrs in the untidy vegetation. The originals of Michelangelo's *Prigioni* are now in the Accademia. The copies are on each side of the grotto; designed as decoration, they were placed in a curtain of crystals and sponges and surrounded by jets of water and strange effects of light. In the second room is the group representing *Paride ed Elena* by Vincenzo de' Rossi. The third room was dominated by the marble white, graceful, and elegant beauty of the *Venere* by Giambologna, which was sculpted in 1570. The goddess bathes, observed with curiosity and desire by four monstrous satyrs clutching the base on which the bath stands. The effects of the water, the hydraulic games, the rustlings and reflections, the rare and fragrant plants have now disappeared, but it is easy to imagine the fascination and amazement of the visitors of long ago.

The second chamber in Buontalenti's grotto with the group of Helen and Paris *by Vincenzo de' Rossi.*

Above and facing page: Two views of the garden at Boboli.

RENAISSANCE AND BAROQUE
VILLAS AND GARDENS

A statue in the garden of villa Garzoni at Collodi, Lucca.

The magnificent villas and gardens of Tuscany have long played a central role in the region's vibrant cultural scene. The stylistic variety evident in their original designs and many transformations reveals much about the local history, economic and political as well as cultural. To understand the significance of the Tuscan villa, we must turn back to the late Middle Ages when the great merchants of the region, the Florentines in particular, invested their capital in the countryside. Slowly drawing power away from the ancient feudal aristocracy, the rising class of merchants displayed their growing influence through the vast country estates they established. They formed a new, wealthy nobility engaged in commerce and open to cultural and artistic innovation.

One of these country estates was the background for the stories of Giovanni Boccaccio's *Decameron*. The group of young men to whom the tales were entrusted fled from Florence and the Black Death of 1348. They took refuge in the beautiful surroundings of a suburban villa whose architectural excellence was admired across the region. The villa, in general, became a place that signified safety from the chaos of urban life—an island, far from the noise, the turmoil that reigned in the overcrowded cities of Italian Middle Ages.

The remarkable rise of the Medici was manifested in the family's purchase and building of villas. The area north of Florence and the Valdarno was their first area of expansion. Cafaggiolo and Il Trebbio were the property of Cosimo il Vecchio, one of the family's most important and powerful early figures. The family was structured along feudal lines, and they recognized the importance of agriculture. Signs of the new mercantile culture can be seen in the Medici's simple gardens, with rustic pergolas resting on brick columns, in which they took their leisure. Careggi, which was nearest to the city, was Lorenzo's favorite, and here he gathered together a circle of intellectuals. It was where he died in 1492.

The Renaissance garden was designed with mathematical precision to create a peaceful refuge. Organized along one central axis, the garden of this era was a haven where classical and Christian civilization joined together in harmony. The crises in Renaissance certainty, the bitter realization that Man did not occupy the center of the cosmos, gave Nature—and its harnessed version, the garden—an increasingly

The main cypress-lined avenue leading to Villa Chigi at Cetinale (Siena).
Following pages: View of the garden of Villa Garzoni at Collodi, Lucca.

important role. The Mannerist garden that followed was designed to surprise the visitor
with metaphysical deceptions and unusual, fantastic visions. In this era, the garden
took on political importance, while the villa underlined the neofeudal change that
was taking place in the grand duchy in the sixteenth century under Cosimo I.

The Medicis continued to acquire a growing number of villas, spread all over the
Tuscan landscape. Their rigorous system of territorial control lent support to their
claims of absolute power in the region. One only has to look at the famous lunettes
by Gustavo Utens to understand the impact of the Medicis' drive to attain dynastic
prestige.

The history of the later baroque period is most evident in the area of Lucca. Here
the self-made nobility who had made their money in the commerce of fabrics found
the breathing room they desired. They created a splendid stage from which to observe
the Europe of Bach and of the birth of modern science. Great botanical collections,
with precious flowers such as tulips imported from the Low Countries, characterized
the opulent gardens of the era. Among those who were commissioned to create these
spectacles, two stand out: Filippo Juvarra, the great Italian architect, and Le Nôtre,
the landscape gardener of Versailles. Of their magnificent creations, only the Villa
Garzoni at Collodi survives in something close to its original form.
In the neoclassical and romantic periods, the baroque and rococo styles gave way
to the park à l'anglais. Camelias in many varieties and tall, exotic plants from Asia
and the New World were introduced in place of the serried ranks of box hedges
that had come before.

The little theatre of Villa La Marlia in Lucca.

*Facing page: House designed by Juvarra
at Villa Garzoni.*

THE AUSTERE SIMPLICITY
OF ARTIMINO

The versatile Bernardo Buontalenti was responsible for the villa at Artimino in Prato. The building was also known as La Ferdinanda after the Medici grand duke who commissioned its construction between 1594 and 1600. It rises in the center of a vast enclosed area set aside for hunting. It is a latter-day fortress in design, buttressed on four sides with ramparts on an escarpment. Originally meant to be a hunting lodge, it is modestly decorated. The loggia has an arrangement of architraves with five spans that open in the center of the western facade. Three big windows open out onto a balcony. The many chimney pots on the roof are an attempt to bring a small sense of play to Buontalenti's austere style. Long gone are the days of the Mannerist fantasy; Buontalenti's terse, dry style reflected the new Medici political approach, the neofeudalism then taking root in Tuscany. There was a chronic lack of water in the area of Artimino, but not even the green seduction of a garden could perturb the compact simplicity and the castle-like appearance of the structure. In 1930 the architect Enrico Lusini added a stairway based on a design attributed to Buontalenti. The flight of stairs is devided into three ramps, two of them curved.

Detail of the decorated fireplace in the villa at Artimino.

On either side of the atrium, two rooms lead to further, adjacent rooms. One of the two was the so-called "public room" or "Salon of the villas," decorated with lunettes by the Flemish painter Giusto Utens representing the various Medici holdings with photographic precision. The loggia "of the Paradises" presents the allegorical work of Domenico Passignano: *Poetry, History, Solicitude, Diligence, Fatigue, Patience.* Beyond a small chapel with religious images, there is more allegorical work in the rooms of Grand Duke Ferdinand with *Heroic Virtue. Obedience, Chastity* and *Fidelity,* on the other hand, were called upon to watch over the Grand Duchess Cristina of Lorraine.

*Facing page: The loggia of the western facade
of the villa at Artimino.*

Two lunettes by Giusto Utens preserved at Artimino and depicting the villas, property of the Medici.

Facing page: Portal of the villa at Artimino, surmounted by the Medici family crest.

POGGIO IMPERIALE

This fascinating villa, with its complex design and history, passed through the hands of various patrician Florentine families before it was confiscated in 1565 by Cosimo de' Medici who gave it to his daughter as part of her dowry. Through her it went to the Odescalchi who sold it in 1622 to Mary Magdalen of Austria, wife of Cosimo II. The grand duchess of Tuscany, proud of her imperial lineage, gave it the name of Poggio Imperiale, setting it aside for future grand duchesses. A competition to enlarge and improve the villa was won by Giulio Parigi. The property later passed to Vittoria della Rovere and then to Grand Duke Leopold of Lorraine, and was further transformed by Gaspare Paoletti, who left the main facade unfinished. The work was completed only in the early nineteenth century by order of Maria Luisa of Bourbon.

The architectural form of the villa at Poggio Imperiale as we see it today is the result of a program of restructuring that began in the Lorraine period and led to a doubling in the size of the building. The main facade underwent many transformations before its ultimate form. The portico of rough ashlar stonework is the work of Pasquale Poccianti, commissioned by Maria Luisa to give the villa that final aspect that Leopold of Lorraine had already planned. The loggia above the portico is the work of Giuseppe Cacialli who freely interpreted the notes and plans left by his predecessor, creating, for instance, a piano nobile in the form of a luminous court surrounded by columns. It is decorated with frescoes and stucco ornaments—the work of Mannelli and Spedulo. Half-columns with Ionic capitals sustain the ample pediment, spaced out with round arches.

Above: Two details of the fresco decoration at the villa at Poggio Imperiale.

Facing page: Facade of the villa.

Following pages: Some of the frescoed and sumptuously furnished chambers at Poggio Imperiale.

VILLA DEL POCCIO IMPERIALE · COLLECIO STATALE DELLA SS · ANNUNZIATA

SURPRISES OF THE SEVENTEENTH-CENTURY
GARDEN AT CASTELLO DI GRICIGLIANO

Detail of the castle grotto faced with

polichrome ceramics.

The Martelli family started the transformation of the Florentine castle of Gricigliano. An old building surrounded by a moat, it was acquired in 1478 by Nicolò d'Ugolino Martelli under the terms of a perpetual lease. From the sixteenth century onwards, a system of plant nurseries—substituting for the moats—and farmhouses was constructed around the edifice. The garden decorations date from the seventeenth century—from the nymphaeum to the stalactite-encrusted arch to the fountain enriched with rustic mosaics on which is mounted a relief of a pelican feeding its young. And finally, the grotto was erected in the eighteenth century. It contained typical Tuscan ceramics such as tartari, traditional containers for grain. The floor was decorated with fragments of porcelain and multicolored ceramics. The chapel, dedicated to St. Joseph, is also of this period.

The severe and compact facades of the residence are decorated only on one side, from which an ample double-naved portico gives access to the central courtyard. The striking, almost feudal geometry of the building, firmly placed on a series of terraces, contrasts with the playful, dynamic series of water basins located at different heights. Connected to each other by small locks or by overflow, they create an amusing sort of canal. A pathway runs parallel to the banks of the water basins. The parapets on the path offer decorated, round stone seats from which there is a view of the greenery and the water of the garden, and an occasional glimpse of the vast hilly landscape that embraces the villa.

Facing page and following pages: Entrance to the castle

at Gricigliano.

THE METAMORPHOSIS OF VILLA CORSI SALVIATI
AT SESTO FIORENTINO

Over the centuries many villas rose on the hills that cluster at the foot of Monte Morello, the privileged hunting area of the Medici, and the marshy plain that lies to the north of Florence. Among these are Petraia and Castello, the emblematic residence of the grand ducal family. The baroque facade of Villa Corsini rises in Castello. In its park, shaded by ilex trees, hides the fountain with the allegorical statue of *River*, sculpted by Tribolo. Atop an imposing Etruscan burial mound, Villa Manfredi a Quinto conserves the tomb of the Montagnola, dating back to the seventh century B.C. Much of the extraordinary natural scenery that attracted the attention of the Macchiaioli painters has been destroyed by the disorderly growth of the Florentine suburbs. But the artistic jewels that are hidden there and the reassuring presence of the Monte Morello still exercise great fascination. In 1502 Simone di Jacopo Corsi bought an estate in the county of San Martino a Sesto. It was Giovanni's son who made the first major improvements on the estate's main house from 1567 to 1569. The heirs of Giovanni Corsi undertook a second phase of transformation between 1593 and 1603. But the definitive metamorphosis of the suburban house into a villa took place between 1632 and 1641 with the enlargement of the main body of buildings and the works in the garden. The vastly expanded structure was crowned by crenellated towers at its four corners. The garden was divided into geometrical sections with a circular basin in the center, and parterres bordered with box hedges, a vegetable garden, a greenhouse for the citrus plants, and a fishpond.

In 1738 Antonio Corsi began work on a new and radical restructuring of the villa. An ornate facade was designed, picked out with a decoration of plaster strips. Turrets in triple form were added. A new central opening in the form of an arch and lateral ones with square lintels were built. Statues crowned the end columns. The two seventeenth-century towers were removed, and a pediment was established on the two floors of the external facade. It was decorated with spirals and crowned by tapered spires, while the various levels were connected by continuous balustrades punctuated with urns and sculptures. It was the garden, however, that underwent the greatest transformation into a baroque set piece. The aviaries were redecorated and connected by a wall that was pierced to reveal an opening enriched with a pediment. The long rectangle of the fishpond was reconfigured and decorated with balusters. The entire garden was populated with statues, basins, and fountains. There was an open-air theatre and the indispensable labyrinth of box hedges, the classic topiary of the Mannerist and Baroque garden. Having undergone this remarkable series of alterations, Villa Corsi now exemplifies the eighteenth-century Tuscan villa.

Two decorative details at Villa Corsi Salviati: Fresco of a grotesque mask and a four-headed lion.

Facing page: Villa garden, decorated with sculptures and terracotta vases.

Rectangular fishpond at Villa Corsi Salviati.

THE BAROQUE FANTASIES
OF VILLA BURLAMACCHI

*Detail of illusionist frescos that decorate the rooms
at Villa Burlamacchi.*

The construction of the compact and severe Villa Burlamacchi at Gattaiola in Lucca
began under its namesake, the patrician Francesco Burlamacchi, around the middle
of the sixteenth century. It was based on a design ascribed to Nicolao Civitali.

There is one open gallery with seven arches on the ground floor. It is cut out of the
facade and softens the prospect that looks over the valley. In 1719 a double ramp
of stairs was added, and in the same period Francesco Antonio Cecchi, the Luccan
painter, decorated it in monochrome with false niches and allegorical statues.
In the seventeenth century, the Santini family came into possession of the villa and
ordered a new, phantasmagoric redecoration. The sedate design of the reception and
family rooms was disturbed. The spaces were transformed and enlarged by illusionary
architectural perspectives. The Santini were followed in the eighteenth century by
the Montecatini, who continued the work in the same style. Bartolomeo de Santi was
among the artists responsible. He painted the false pilasters, supplementary arches,
urns, garlands, sculptures, aerial balconies and galleries stretching up to limpid and
radiant skies. The skies themselves are crossed by allegorical representations of Time,
the graceful figures of Dawn and Spring, and by a splendid Chariot of the Sun.
Then there are the baroque balusters that penetrate the ceilings and open up fantastical
Arcadian landscapes as backdrops for the bucolic passages and knightly scenes taken
from Torquato Tasso's *Jerusalem Liberated*.

The inventive excess of this tide of pictorial decoration must have fascinated the
nineteenth-century owner of the villa, Count Alfred Emilien de Nieuwerkerke.
A refined, worldly figure, in addition to being a sculptor, he was the eclectic director
general of France's state museums, the organizer of the famous "Fridays at the Louvre,"
and later superintendent of the Ècole des Beaux-Arts during the Second Empire.

*Facing page: The loggia on the ground floor
of the villa, decorated with monochrome frescos
by Francesco Antonio Checchi.
Following pages: Room decorated with illusionist
architecture and the villa library.*

LIGURIAN ARCHITECTURE RECALLED
AT VILLA MALASPINA
AT CANIPAROLA DI FOSDINOVO

Around 1720, Carlo Agostino Malaspina, Marchese of Fosdinovo, and his son
Gabriello decided to build a villa around the previous site of an ancient tower at
Caniparola di Fosdinovo in Massa Carrara. The elegant main facade, enriched
with bright color, is laid out in peculiar fashion. There is a masonry separation
in the center that divides the two parallel sides. Three decreasing parts of the prospect,
grafted to the base plinth, give a dynamic lift to the architectural composition, which
is otherwise all on the horizontal. On the small strip of the attic, the central pediment
widens and joins together in two elongated spirals. A careful examination of the facade
reveals the intelligence of the plan. It can be seen in the sophistication of the
proportions, of the overhangs, the wooden window casings set back to the mezzanine
floor. The barrel vault in the middle of the loggia is more spacious. The deep loggia
accentuates the light and shade and the two dimensionality of the design.
In direct contrast to the Tuscan formality that distinguishes the design of the facade,
the lively coloring of the exterior plaster is a legacy of the architectural tradition
of nearby Liguria, an ancient border territory and crossroads of many cultures.

Detail of frescoed ceiling at Villa Malaspina.

Facade with double ramped stairway and frescoed loggia

at Villa Malaspina.

Following pages: Two internal rooms at the villa, with walls decorated in baroque and illusionist architecture and seventeenth- and eighteenth-century furniture.

THE WINDING BAROQUE STAIRCASE
OF VILLA LA TANA

View of the valley from the balustrade of Villa La Tana.

The ancient property upon which rises Villa La Tana at Candeli, opening wide on the Florentine plain, is lapped by a branch of the Arno river near the fishery of Le Viaccie. The estate can be traced back to the Bucelli family, who sold it in 1548 to the Landi family. In 1579 it passed from them into the hands of Piero di Zanobi Bonaventuri, the indulgent husband of Bianca Cappello. When he died, in 1574, he bequeathed the "grand house" to her, and she was at last free to acquire the grand ducal crown. The name of Bianca, a Venetian noblewoman and mistress of Francesco I de' Medici, was forever linked to the property. In 1631 the Ricasoli family, to whom the property had descended, undertook a vast program of transformation and enlargement. The existing edifice had been called "La Tana" ("The Lair") for its location, described by one historian as "almost hidden, buried among the woods that entirely covered the slopes of the knoll, l'Incontro." The Ricasoli conferred on the house the dignity of a villa. In 1740 Leon Francesco Pasquale Ricasoli commissioned a particularly striking series of alterations to the residence, situated in a dominating position on the side of a hill. The architect that he chose was Giulio Foggini, brother of the more famous Giovan Battista, master of the ornate, extreme baroque style favored by the Medici.

Under Foggini, the structure was enlarged with two lateral wings, while in the center an attic pediment crowned the body of the main building. The villa rises like a backdrop at the end of a theatrical and imposing composition of ramps that introduce a broad, jutting flight of stairs. Two graceful curving arms enclose the grotto that opens at the center of the retaining wall, from which rise another two ramps winding straight up. The symmetrical pairs of statues that decorate the system of stairways accentuate the sense of solemnity as one approaches the villa. The stairways, added in the eighteenth century to provide a powerful feeling of upward movement, open onto a terraced belvedere that overlooks the landscape towards Florence. Nineteenth-century modifications have altered the main facade of La Tana; the formal garden, designed in geometric parterres and boxwood recesses, also shows the influence of this era.

Facing and following pages: Facade of the villa with the winding staircase decorated with eighteenth-century statuary.

SCENIC DESIGN OF VILLA BIANCHI BANDINELLI AT GEGGIANO

Ranuccio Bianchi Bandinelli Paparoni, a gentleman of Siena, received as a dowry from his first wife Gerolama Santi a farm property with adjoining living quarters situated at Geggiano near Siena. In 1729 he decided to restore the villa by uniting the various parts of the old buildings, adding a room to the left wing, and opening loggias (now walled up) on both flanks. Today, however, the visual aspect of the villa is almost entirely the product of work done between 1768 and 1769. The principal facade is a structure of pilaster strips intersected at the height of the second floor by a large horizontal band that defines the parallel lines of the string-course and those of the parapet of the apertures. The exterior is not a creation of particular originality, but the interior, redecorated between 1780 and 1790, is of great interest. Here the Rocaille and the rising neoclassical style come together. The walls of the "green room" are covered with tapestries representing farm work and seasonal allegories in opulent Baroque borders. In the long entrance gallery is a fresco, *Allegorie dei Mesi*, by Ignas Moder, Tyrolean by birth but Sienese by choice. The splendid furnishings are also worthy of note. Designed by the Sienese neoclassical architect Agostino Fantastici at the beginning of the nineteenth century, they are a kind of Italian updating of Schinkel. The Italian garden begins below the great square facing the villa. Within the garden is an eighteenth-century open-air theater, against a background of greenery. The proscenium is composed of arches crowned with classical pediments, emblazoned with the coats of arms of Bianchi Bandinelli and Chigi Zondadari. On the diagonal walls two niches enclose allegorical statues of *Commedia* and *Tragedia*, works by the Maltese sculptor Bosio. The garden is protected by a high wall in which there are six theatrical gates flanked by monumental pilasters topped by pyramids in carved frames. The gates are decorated with two-handled urns and mocking rococo statues of Barbary apes. With its theatrical spirit, Geggiano caught the fancy of film director Bernardo Bertolucci, who used the villa to shoot some of the dream sequences and other significant scenes of his film *Io ballo da sola* (*Stealing Beauty*).

Detail of tapestry in "toile de Jouy" on the walls of a room in the villa.

Facing page: Fresco of Allegories of the Months by the Tyrolean painter Ignaz Moder, in the entrance gallery of the villa.
Following pages: One of the gates of the villa with pillars surmounted by apes.

CURIOUS MUSEUMS
OF ART, MAGIC, AND SCIENCE

The museums of Tuscany are an integral part of that inimitable fascination the region holds for tourists, for enthusiasts and lovers of art from around the world. The very name of Uffizzi brings to mind Botticelli, Raffaello, Andrea del Sarto; the Florentine Galleria dell'Accademia, dominated by the gigantic sculpture of David, is the destination of thousands of visitors every year; the same is true of the Pitti as well. And beyond these, there are other museums, both large and small, that are unexpectedly beautiful, places that convey a sense of timelessness and evoke profound emotions.

The Museo dell'Opera del Duomo in Florence, for example, is on a par with the more famous institutions just mentioned. It lies at the center of a galaxy of remarkable art collections connected to parish chapels, churches and monasteries scattered all over the territory of Tuscany. Among the many other museums worthy of a visit is the Museo d'Arte Sacra of the Collegiata di Asciano, those of the diocese of Pienza (with the famous parish church of Pio II Piccolomini), and that of Montalcino. They are all in the tradition of the Siena school, amongst the most splendid and least remarked jewels of Tuscany.

To return to the Florentine area and the secular, among the greatest Medici splendors is the Museum of Silver in Palazzo Pitti. This true chamber of wonders throws open the grand ducal coffers and amazes with an almost obsessive opulence. The eclectic and transfigured dream of an nineteenth-century collector still vibrates in the picturesque rooms of Villa Stibbert. The paintings of Bartolomeo Bimbi capture the spirit of a baroque grand duchy suspended between neofeudalism, pious cant and new, revolutionary science and technology. Then there is the strange unsettled feeling that overcomes the visitor to La Specola, especially as one looks at the macabre wax figures of Zumbo, or the precise sophistication and hyperrealism of the wax models in the Botanical Museum. And lastly, there are the sublime groups of marble, bronze, and terracotta sculptures of the Bargello and their near-opposites, the pure white ghosts of gesso at the Florentine Gipsoteca and those in the Accademia. Here, in serried ranks, busts, bas reliefs, and sculptures retrace the neoclassical work of the great Lorenzo Bartolini.

Facing page: A room of the Museo dell'Opera of the Duomo in Pisa.

THE MARVELS
OF THE MUSEO DEGLI ARGENTI

Above: Details of sea horses from the Medici collection.
Facing page: A room of the Museo degli Argenti.

Following page from top to bottom: Onyx cameo
portrait of Pope Clement VII; Calcedon and agate
cameo depicting Hercules; Cameo portrait of Cosimo
II; at right: Cameo depicting a Medici family group.

Page 101: Inlay medallion by Bernardino Gaffuri
depicting Piazza della Signoria in Florence.

The Museo degli Argenti, or Museum of Silver, is a fascinating, intellectually seductive place, a marvelous chamber of wonders crowded with objects that bring to life ancient passions and glorious stories of love and power. The museum reveals the opulence, the magnificent extravagance that exemplified the visual style of Europe's courts from the era of Mannerism through the baroque. The treasure of the prince-bishops of Salzburg, which it houses, was brought to the capital of the grand duchy by Ferdinando III of Lorraine at the beginning of the nineteenth century. Among the museum's other treasures is a collection of amber, glass, and ivory previously in the museum at the Bargello, the Gabinetto delle Gemme degli Uffizi. There is also a significant collection of jewels bequeathed to the city of Florence at the beginning of the eighteenth century by the last descendant of the Medici, the electress of Palatine, Anna Ludovica, who was responsible for the preservation of much of the artistic patrimony of Florence.

Along the rooms that were once the summer quarters of the grand duke, stretching to what seems like infinity, there is a stunning series of goblets and vases of rock crystal or lapis lazuli and gold, of Medici cameos, of mosaics in semiprecious stones, of jewel caskets and reliquaries, of ivories. This breathtaking collection is heaped together like some pirates' fabulous booty, or like the treasures in Ali Baba's cave. The collection of polished ivory goblets, exceptional in its refinement, was part of the war booty of a victorious campaign conducted in Germany by Mattias de' Medici during the bloody Thirty Years War of the fifteenth century. The famous Stipo di Alemagna, which today is in the center of the Throne Room, was once among the rarities held in the Tribune of the Uffizi. The Tribune is also immortalized in the renowned, minutely detailed sixteenth-century painting by John Zoffany. A sumptuous cabinet was offered in 1628 by the archduke of Tyrol, Leopold of Hapsburg, as a gift to the grand duke Ferdinando II. It was made for the occasion by the highly skilled Bavarian artisans of Augusta. Inside there are a series of compartments enriched in Florentine mosaics and worked in amber. While classically proportioned, it is dizzyingly ornate, every detail covered with semiprecious stones in designs characteristic of the late Mannerist period. It seems to incarnate the magnificent decadence of the Age of the Medici, the slow death of that dynasty amidst baroque ceremonies and religious bigotry, alchemy, and magic, even as the world was being transformed by the scientific investigations and discoveries of Torricelli, Redi and Galileo.

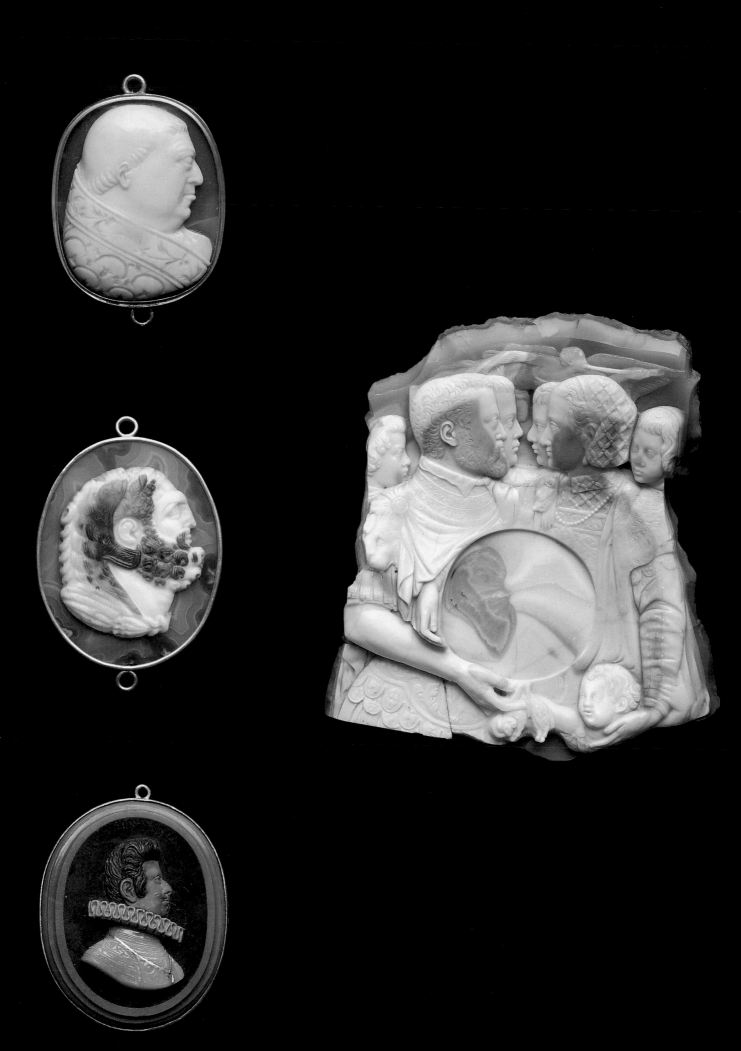

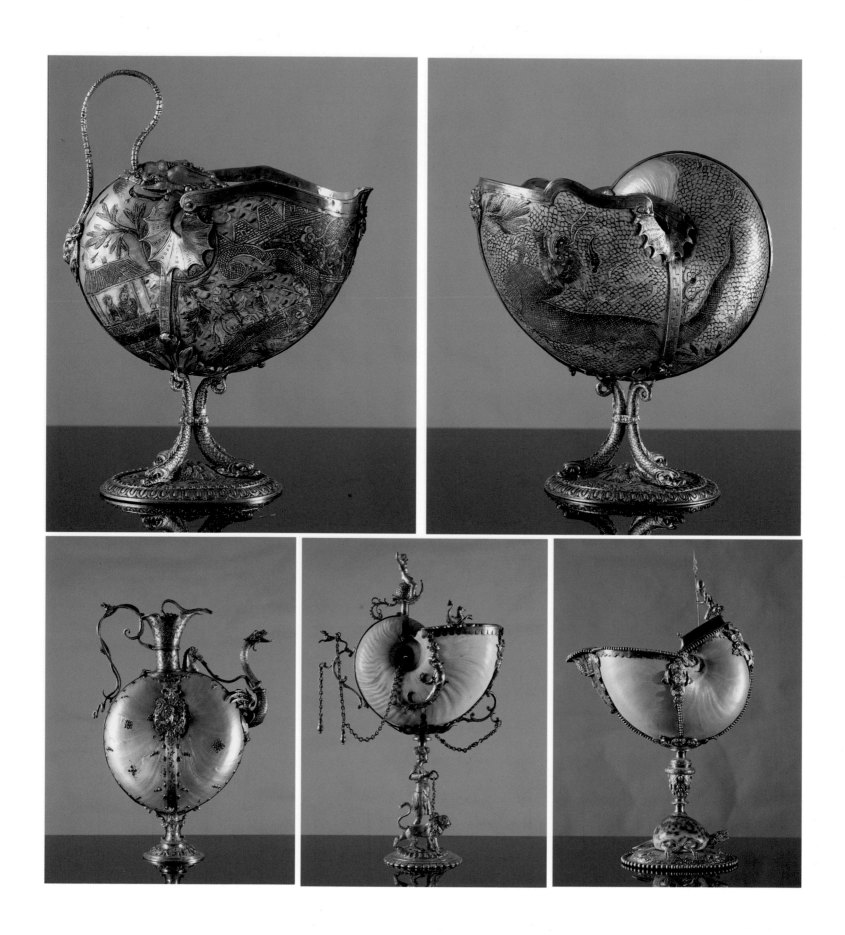

Above and facing page: Rock crystal vase and some examples of the nautilus collection encrusted with precious stones and metals, from the Medici collection.

1. S. Giouanni
2. S. Bartola
3. Appiola
4. Appiolona
5. Appiola lunga rossa
6. Re appiola
7. Vinoña
8. Panaia rossa
9. Renetta bastarda
10. Panaia bianca
11. Rosa
12. Regina
13. Tedesca
14. Poppina
15. Bugnola
16. Curpauda grigia
17. Carouella
18. Madresina
19. Violata
20. Franchetti
21. Dolce
22. Rossa
23. Francesca
24. Francesca rigata
25. Silia
26. Musa
27. A Spicchi
28. Reine Damine
29. Cacciuola

30. Appiola di Francia
31. Paradise
32. Zuccherine
33. Testa
34. Ruggine
35. Paradisa rossa
36. Manza
37. Bocca preua
38. Rossa di Lunigiana
39. Baccalare
40. Comusa
41. Grossa
42. Fior di Cassia
43. S. Signora
44. S. Piera
45. Sciampion
46. Dolce di Francia
47. Martin secco di Spagna
48. Diacciata
49. Martin peres
50. Lazzeruola
51. Appiolona rossa
52. Lunga

Bimbi 1696

THE DELIGHTS OF THE TUSCAN BOTANICAL
GARDEN IN THE PAINTINGS
OF BARTOLOMEO BIMBI

*Detail of the work of Bartolomeo Bimbi held in the villa
at Poggio Caiano.*

During the late seventeenth and early eighteenth centuries, the era of Cosimo III
de' Medici, there was also a great fashion for collecting botanical rarities from both the
New World and the Old. These delicacies, gathered from orchards and kitchen gardens
alike, graced the grand ducal table. The villa at Poggio a Caiano preserves a series of
paintings by Bartolomeo Bimbi that are a testimony to the abundance, the variety, the
exuberant color of these mouth-watering fruits, each of whose names are painstakingly
displayed on the painted canvases.

Bartolomeo Bimbi, a Florentine painter, was born in 1648, and died in the city in 1730.
A pupil of Lorenzo Lippi and Onorio Marinari, he worked side-by-side with the
naturalist and scholar Francesco Redi. With his soft, thick brushwork he gave life to
an amazing collection of fruits which look almost ready to be eaten. They are set like
precious jewels in the stunning baroque gilded wood frames carved by the Dutch master
of intaglio, Vittorio Crosten. The colors are brilliant—the fleshy range of reds from
magenta to wine, the yellow of the lemons that contrasts with the livid purple of the
plums, the ruby of the velvets, the pink apricots, all stand out against the stormy, blue,
baroque skies, and are reflected in the luxurious gold of the frames. There is fruit, like
the incredible 111 varieties of pears with fabulous, exotic names; muscadines, tiny
orange-, butter-, and bergamot-pears; a cornucopia that pours out bunches of perfumed
grapes—those same vines that Redi enthuses over in his *Bacco in Toscana*; ripe and
colorful apples, cherries, plums, cherubs pouring water, majestic trophies of figs.
In harmony with the painted subjects, the superb gilded frames that surround them
continue the theme of luxurious, almost carnal overgrowth. Swarming with fruit and
flowers, they are sculpted with an incredible virtuosity. The entire series of paintings,
originally destined for the Casino della Topaia, near the villa di Castello, constitutes
an epic poem for Pomona, the ancient Roman goddess of fertility, and still evokes the
princely splendor of the last Medici.

Above and facing page: Paintings by Bimbi

in the original gold baroque wood frames carved

by the engraver Vittorio Crosten.

Following pages: Various qualities of figs in a painting

by Bartolomeo Bimbi.

Fichi Primaticci
1 Palquati   11 Verdini
2 S. Giovanni   12 Rigati di Marsilia
3 Zuccaiolo di Lunigiana   13 Calauresi
4 Monacci primaticci   14 Bragioti
5 Albi primaticci   15 Rossetti
6 Dottato primaticcio   16 Durachi
7 Gamoncino di Marsilia   17 Lampa. Portughese
8 S. Piero   18 Bragratti
9 Napoletano

Fichi Settentrini
1. Albi
2. Rossellini dell'Vrigiana
3. Verdini Bianchi
4. Dottati saluatici & Auig.
5. Pisabello
6. Brogiotto Bianco
7. Lardello
8. Garzoncino
9. S. Maria
10. Piernotto Romano
11. San pieru
12. Castagnino
13. Sodino
14. Nardo
15. Cehin
16. Caualier
17. Parali
18. Ros
19. Fioun
20. Brogiotti
21. Verdon
22. Laulaui
23. Rondon Piano
24. Cordolin
25. Dell Pernun
26. Catagnioli Rossellini
27. Lardon
28. Correttione

AGOSTO

a. 2. Roffelletta   17. Roffellet: piccola.
pana verde   18. Becco d'Oca chiara
cellicra   19. Gagliotta rofata
m:bian:d'Eftate   20. Il Verde
letta   21. Zucchero verde

SETTEMBRE
1. Gatto-abbruciata
2. Martin fecco

OTTOBRE
1. Vergolofa.   2. Fanal
3. Guidall'. 4. Luifa bu
5. Norgall' 6. Duraz

Detail of a painting by Bartolomeo Bimbi depicting
one hundred and eleven varieties of pears, catalogued
according to their ripening season.

Within the lower-left detail, the painted inscription reads:

Zucca nata in Pisa
nel Giardino di S.AR.
detto di S. Francesco
...1711 Pesaua 8160.

Details from paintings of fruit and vegetables
by Bartolomeo Bimbi from the collection of Cosimo III
de' Medici.

EXOTIC WAX PLANTS
AT THE BOTANICAL MUSEUM IN FLORENCE

The Botanical Institute of Florence includes a school, the gardens, and a museum. The Florentine Botanical Gardens have a glorious past. They were founded by the grand duke Cosimo I de' Medici in 1545 and called the Giardino dei Semplici. One of the first such gardens in Europe, they were most likely preceded only by a similar institution in Padova and by that of the Arsenale of Pisa, also founded by the Medici.

From the sixteenth century on, and particularly after the discovery of the New World encouraged the introduction of new botanical species, the Medici were always alive to the potential for developing new plants. They were just as proud and insatiable as collectors of botanical rarities as they were of works of art and precious objects. North of Florence, the Medici villa at Castello became a place dedicated to botanical experiments, and in particular to citrus fruits of which an astounding variety was cultivated. These, along with the precious orris root which was a speciality of Tuscany, were also among the basic ingredients of the art of perfumery, practiced in the region as far back as the High Middle Ages.

Details of wax models of Hedichium *and* Fritillaria.

The Botanical Museum of Florence is the most important in Italy. It was founded in 1776 by the grand duke Pietro Lepoldo of Lorraine, and is now entrusted to the naturalist Felice Fontana. It is now part of the University and includes a rich display of wood, with thousands of different specimens. A herbarium founded in the mid-nineteenth century and containing numerous collections has a total of four million species of herbs dating from the sixteenth and eighteenth centuries. A tropical herbarium that is also part of the museum houses a noteworthy collection of examples from the former Italian colonies of Eritrea, Somalia, and Ethiopia in East Africa.

Among the collections of various botanical specimens, one of the most interesting is an nineteenth-century collection of wax models of exotic plants. Mounted in neoclassical vases made by Ginori, they have been admired by many, including the great Bonaparte. The local wax modelling school has its origins between the thirteenth and fourteenth centuries. By the seventeenth century it was specializing in models for the purpose of scientific education. Because the Roman Church forbade the dissection of cadavers, the school had the opportunity to pursue and achieve remarkably lifelike results.

Facing page: Wax models of Jacquinia *and* Aloe *made by Clemente Susini, with ceramic vases manufactured by Ginori.*

Following pages: Models of Plumeria, Calceolaria, Fritillaria, *and* Pyrus japonica.

A number of extraordinary artists contributed to the formation of the singular collection of the Botanical Museum. There was Clemente Susini, who in the late eighteenth century made the first models of exotic vegetables, and his successor Francesco Calenzuoli. The most famous was Luigi Calamai, who lived in the first half of the nineteenth century. Egisto Tortori continued the work of Calamai from 1841 under the guidance of the notable botanist Filippo Parlatore. Tortori specialized in microscopic models, among which the most important was the reproduction of the attack of the dreaded fungus Uncinula Necator, enemy of the grapevine, that in 1852 seriously damaged the viticulture of Tuscany.

THE ZOOLOGICAL COLLECTIONS
OF LA SPECOLA

The ancient palazzo Torrigiani houses the Tribune of Galileo on the first floor.
It was built in 1841 at the orders of Leopoldo II of Lorraine for the Congress of Italian
Scientists, and the second floor is the headquarters of the Zoological Museum of
Florence, called La Specola because the grand duke Pietro Leopoldo had created there
an astronomical and meteorological observatory. Besides its fascinating zoological
collections, the museum is worthy of interest for its collection of anatomical models
in wax. These were made in the wax laboratories in the annex created in the second
half of the eighteenth century and operational until 1895. The work of Clemente
Susini who modeled them under the guidance of the famous anatomist Felice Fontana,
these anatomical models are enlivened by their fascination with the grotesque. Part of
the legacy of the science of the baroque age, they seem to be inspired by a pleasure with
the crude representation of the most horrible and pitiless details of human morphology,
of the most detailed examination of diseases and infections. It is a bewitching and
terrible fascination that echoes in the pages of the celebrated Mario Praz, and in the
dense and almost cinematographic depiction of the so-called Plagues of Zumbo.
The museum also holds collections of games designed to ward off the evil eye and
ex-votos crowded with wax figures. Fashioned with incredible mastery, they represent
the devastating effects of one of the greatest recurring epidemics of the seventeenth
century that struck three different Italian cities.

Detail of a room forming part of the zoological collection in the museum.

Showcases with anatomical models in wax made in the wax laboratories annexed to the museum and active since the second half of the eighteenth century.

Case showing various species of starfish.

One of the rooms given over to the zoological collection.

THE GLORIES OF THE PAST
IN THE DREAMS OF FEDERICO STIBBERT

Federico Stibbert dedicated his entire adult life to building a collection of objects
that could reconstruct the Florence of the past, at least as imagined through the prism
of nineteenth-century English fancies concerning the city in the heyday of its Medici
splendor. Beginning in 1860 this Anglo-Italian collector gathered together in his
Florentine villa a variegated body of objects ranging from paintings to fabrics, sculpture
to weaponry, with the intention of recreating the splendor of an idealized past. Of the
Stibbert Museum's many holdings, the section dedicated to weaponry is perhaps the
most interesting and complete. Through sixty-four rooms a collection of both Western
and Eastern weapons and armor unfolds that is considered among the most important
of its kind in the world. There are complete suits of armor from mid-fourteenth century
Europe, Japanese armor of the seventeenth and eighteenth centuries, Persian and
Indian swords, and Greek and Roman weapons. There are incredible series of dirks,
daggers, swords, dress-swords, scimitars, lances, knives, crossbows, padded sheaths,
harquebuses, carbines, catapults and other arms that stretch through the rooms of the
villa following a plan more picturesque than systematic in intent. The most suggestive
of the rooms is that of "the cavalry charge." Here in a luxuriance of panoplies, standards
and wall decorations of fantastic Gothic inspiration, twenty-four horsemen and
fourteen infantrymen fully decked out in the armor and weapons of the age file past,
their horses covered with caparisons flaunting proud heraldic decorations. Even if the
cortege depicts an historic farrago, with German soldiers depicted alongside Saracens,
Spaniards with Italians, this epic parade of horsemen makes a powerful impression.
The approach is almost cinematographic, and it would certainly have pleased Stibbert,
locked in the splendid dream of his villa, among gold-encrusted leathers, baroque
furniture, and splendid Renaissance paintings; an alternative, perhaps, to gazing
out from the Venetian loggia of flowery Gothic ogival arches that open on to the
broad park below.

*One of the suits of armor preserved in the Stibbert
museum.*

*Facing page: The "Riders' Room" with a range
of horsemen and infantry in full costume.
Following pages: Dining room on the ground floor,
with a seventeenth-century Italian harpsichord
and a table of the same period.*

Left and facing page: "Egyptian" temple and
"Venetian" loggia with flowered Gothic ogives,
overlooking the large park that surrounds the museum.

THE PLASTER CASTS OF MASTERPIECES
IN THE GIPSOTECA IN FLORENCE

A gathering of white ghosts populates the roomy chambers of the great Gipsoteca in Florence. They are plaster casts of many of Europe's great sculptural masterpieces. Originally intended for teaching purposes, they now comprise a museum collection of immense fascination. The Gipsoteca was created at the Preparatory School of Intaglio and Applied Arts, founded in 1869 in the cloisters of Santa Croce. Its support came from private citizens among whom number some of the most illustrious names of the age, including Baron Franchetti, Marchese Torrigiani, the architect Poggi, Vittorio Alinari, and Carlo Brogi. Soon after its founding, the school set out to create a collection of plaster casts of famous sculptures, intended as models for the students.

In 1887, many plaster casts were exhibited together with the originals during the festivities celebrating Donatello. In many cases the casts were the work of the professors of the School of Santa Croce who donated them to the institution. By the end of the nineteenth century, the collection also included the plaster casts of Angelo Giannini of Siena, and the Florentine Oronzio Lelli, whose work was continued by his sons. In 1919 one of Lelli's sons, Luigi, sold his rich collection consisting of about two thousand pieces to the School. In fact, in that year the School became an Institute and was transferred to the larger premises of what used to be the royal stables in the Giardino della Pace at Porta Romana. In 1929 Luigi Lelli was employed as an art teacher at the Gipsoteca, and later became its first curator.

Above, facing page, and following pages:
Details of the plaster casts of the masterpieces
of the Classical and Renaissance ages and collected
in the Gipsoteca of the Accademia.

The casts survived the wars of this century and have been joined by new acquisitions. Among these are the forms of Giotto's campanile, the reliefs of the Arch of Trajan in Benevento, the most important Romanesque monuments in Puglia, and the sarcophagi of San Vitale and Sant'Apollinare in Ravenna. One can enjoy unusual glimpses of the history of art in the halls of the Gipsoteca. Donatello's *Gattamelata* on horseback converses with *Eleonora of Aragon* by Laurana. Elsewhere the works of Rossellino, of Verrocchio, of Benedetto da Maiano, are neighbor to Giambologna's *Mercurio*. The modern need to substitute many originals in order to save them from the decay caused by atmospheric pollution, and an increase in demand from private sources, have led to continued production of the plaster casts. The most acclaimed remain the classics of antiquity and of the Renaissance, Donatello and Michelangelo prized above all.

TUSCANY
AND THE *FIN-DE-SIÈCLE*

The glories of Tuscan art and culture are not limited to the Renaissance. In the twilight of the centennial magnificence of Medici power, a controlled and classical baroque style produced extraordinary results. But it was probably upon the arrival of the Lorraine, and particularly from the end of the eighteenth century into the beginning of the nineteenth century that the Grand Duchy became the privileged location of experiments in science and artistic philosophy. The new century opened with the visionary architectural imaginism and the Gothic style of Agostino Fantastici of Siena and with the industrial Gothic Revival of Alessandro Gherardesca. The sculpture of Lorenzo Bartolini recalled the poetry of Foscolo. The Gothic Revival that began in England during the eighteenth century, due in large part to Horace Walpole's Strawberry Hill, spread all over Europe during the course of the next hundred years. Among those artists responsible were Viollet-le-Duc in France, Pugin in England, and Jappelli and Boito in Italy. The Englishman John Ruskin bore the standard, proclaiming the lost purity of Gothic architecture.

The nineteenth century also saw the birth of an idealized conception of Tuscany, as imagined and seen through the eyes and often morbid sensibility of the *grand touristes* and of the crowded and diverse Anglo-Franco-American colony that had established itself among the villas and the hills around Florence. This intellectual and cosmopolitan world of expatriates is described in the pages of Henry James, of Vernon Lee, and of Mario Praz. It was inexorably swept away by World War II.

Facing page: Egyptian inspired decoration by Agostino Fantastici in Villa Il Pavone in Siena.

MEMORIES OF THE NAPOLEONIC EPIC
AT VILLA NAPOLEONE-DEMIDOFF
ON THE ISLAND OF ELBA

During his brief exile on Elba, Napoleon settled in the little house of the Mulini and in the small villa at Portoferraio, a two-storied building that had once been a farm house. The villa's lower floor was occupied by the bathrooms and included the so-called Bath of Paolina, decorated with images of intertwining, climbing plants against the background of a dark sky. Paolina was the generous, extravagant younger sister of the Roman emperor, wife of the prince Camillo Borghese, and depicted as the *Victorious Venus* in the famous marble sculpture by Antonio Canova. The upper floor of the structure was turned into residential and reception rooms. Bonaparte and the dignitaries of his small court-in-exile took up residence. Here, in the center of the square plan of the building, is the villa's Egyptian room, the walls decorated with a *Return from Egypt* with hieroglyphs in false bas-reliefs. An airy loggia overlooks a fantastic landscape. The decoration in the bedroom recalls the more fortunate times of Napoleon's military and political career. A *trompe l'oeil* of elegantly draped curtains brings to mind an officer's field tent.

After falling into disuse for a short period, the villa at San Martino was bought in 1851 by the Russian prince Anatolij Demidoff, who was related to Bonaparte. He proposed transforming the villa into a place dedicated to the Napoleonic epic and collected mementos and testimonies. The prince had the architect Nicola Matas design a grandiose galleried edifice, a sort of museum that would incorporate the original building. The Napoleonic myth found its sanctuary in this pavilion in the form of a temple with projecting wings. The building is ornamented with a Doric frieze and sculpted eagles, emblematic of the Napoleonic cult. The building spreads horizontally on high ground, on an axis with the villa behind. The form of the building is that of a propylaeum or entrance to a temple intended as a filter and a sacred introduction to the villa itself. The building was finished in 1856 and three years later was opened to the public. There is a collection of manuscripts, bronzes, ceramics, busts of the Imperial family, etchings and paintings by Gérard and Horace Vernet. The whole is watched over by Canova's marble statue of the matriarch Letizia Ramolino Bonaparte. Only twenty years after its establishment, Anatoliji Demidoff's nephew put the entire contents of the museum up for auction, putting an end to the invocation of the glorious Napoleonic era.

Napoleonic coats of arms on the exterior walls of Villa Napoleone-Demidoff on the island of Elba.

Facing page: Reception room in Villa Napoleone-Demidoff with Egyptian inspired fresco decorations on the walls.
Following pages: Exterior of the building designed by Nicola Matas and other two rooms in the villa.

THE CASTLE OF BROLIO
FROM THE MIDDLE AGES
TO THE RISORGIMENTO

Detail of neomedieval decoration in the castle at Brolio.

Amid the ordered geometry of the hills of Chianti, the castle of Brolio rises in stark contrast to the vast blue of the Tuscan sky and the dark green of the cypresses, the pines, and the holm oaks that surround it. Named for a prestigious family that traces its history in the region back to 1141, the story of the castle reaches its greatest moments in the period of the Risorgimento. Wine production, for which the name of Brolio is famous, has always been a central part of that history. The building as seen today is the result of various transformations, culminating in a last, fanciful Gothic Revival restoration impressed upon it by the architect Pietro Marchetti from Siena by will of Bettino Ricasoli, the famous statesman.

The feudal castle dominates the surrounding area from an isolated hill, posed on the southern dorsal of Chianti. The castle's long and varied history—from the time when it played a formidable role in the Florentine wars of the fifteenth and sixteenth centuries to the time when it was inhabited in the nineteenth century—can be seen in the various constructions of the castle surroundings, the formal gardens, and the green forests. Brolio was often at the center of armed conflict, as when it was taken by Pandolfo Petrucci of Siena in 1478. The Florentines were responsible for the castle's reconstruction in 1484 and controlled it until 1529 when, taking advantage of the imperial siege of the City of the Fleur-de-lis, the Sienese repossessed it and partially burned it down. After the final end to the Republic of Siena in 1559, there were centuries of relative obscurity under the dominion of the Grand Duchy. The castle's fraught history was symbolically redeemed in the nineteenth century by Siena's entry into the new Kingdom of Italy and by the decisive contribution of Bettino Ricasoli to the formation of an Italian nation that would transcend petty parochialism.

Marchetti's revenge was the reconstruction of the castle, giving it a Gothic feeling that is tied closely to local history and chosen for its romantic and sentimental value. Brickwork is the essential component of the architecture of Siena's great republican revival—Palazzo Pubblico is an example. Bricks were chosen in polemic antithesis to the stone that is the characteristic feature of Florentine buildings. Marchetti pursues a symbolic expression of the civic with his repertory of trifors, towers, battlements, and elegantly ornamental arches scattered throughout the castle. In the interior of the main building there is a labyrinth of rooms and chambers that betray their Renaissance

Facing page: Exterior of the castle with crowning crenellation.

decorative origin through the fashionable imaginative historicism of the nineteenth century. There is a measured, human scale to the reception rooms as well as those set apart for more private use, such as the library containing thousands of rare volumes and dominated by a portrait of the famous Baron Bettino, who died at the castle in 1880.

A series of reception rooms wind their way from the main entrance over two floors. An unbridled architectural inventiveness informs every single piece of furniture and decoration, every wall. The dining room is a panoply of neomedieval symbols, triumphant with battle standards, flags flying, evoking the Age of Chivalry. Great Flemish arrasses, French armor, walls with fine inlay, decorated ceiling beams, plaster ogives, allegorical portraits, heavily ornamented balconies, colored leaded glass studded with coats of arms fill the room—an excessive riot of the material that achieves an almost sacred power. Marchetti himself designed the great, solemn central table, and the fantastically faux-Gothic chairs.

Castle library with portrait of Bettino Ricasoli, and the living room with coffered ceiling.
Facing page and following pages: Castle dining room with neogothic frescos, banners and reconstructions of antique suits of armor.

REMEMBRANCE OF FAMOUS PEOPLE
AT THE GREAT PUCCINI VILLA AT SCORNIO

Niccolò Puccini was an early nineteenth-century patrician from Pistoia. He was often placed under surveillance by the police of the grand duchy for his liberal and revolutionary sympathies. The Medici by this time had been succeeded on the throne of Florence by the Hapsburg-Lorraine part of the reigning family of Austria after the Congress of Vienna. The gauntlet of patriotism and free thought was cast by Puccini not least through his artistic patronage. For the study of his palazzo in the city he commissioned paintings of Dante and Petrarch, of Boccaccio and Machiavelli, spiritual guardians of Italian national culture and champions of unification. The room also contained portraits of eighteenth-century heroes of the French and American revolutions such as Franklin, Washington, and Lafayette.

In 1824 he inherited from Tommaso Puccini the eighteenth-century villa of Scornio, the interior of which had been decorated by Gian Domenico Ferretti and Niccolò Lapi, and restored at the beginning of the nineteenth century by Cosimo Rossi Melocchi. Seeking to awaken patriotic sentiments, Puccini undertook a program to erect a series of evocative and provocative monuments in the garden. In 1838 Puccini asked Alessandro Gherardesca to design a "Pantheon of Illustrious Men" and erect busts, memorial stones, columns and commemorative sculptures in honor of illustrious men of strong will, Italian artists, and advocators of nationalism and self-rule. Among these were Dante, Michelangelo, Colombus, Raffaello, Francesco Ferrucci—the sixteenth-century hero of the anti-Imperial Florentine resistance, Machiavelli, Galileo, Torquato Tasso, the historian Giambattista Vico, Botta, the neoclassic sculptor Antonio Canova. The monumental portraits of this sociopolitical metaphor of a garden were joined by allegorical structures, neomedieval in form: the Tower of Catlinia (symbolizing Warning), the Gothic Castle (Memory), the Romitorio (Training), the Gothic Basilica (Faith).

Details of eighteenth-century decoration inside the villa.

The little temple dedicated to Pythagoras at the palazzo underscores Puccini's eccentric taste for pagan rituals. The temple was first designed by Giuseppe Martelli in 1836 and was erected on an artificial island in the middle of the palazzo's lake.

In addition to the influence he exercised as a patron of the arts, Puccini was a generous philanthropist. Among his various projects, he founded a nursery school and the School at Ponte Napoleone. In 1841 he instituted an annual festival dedicated to "the ears of corn." It was both a meeting place and market for farmers and an occasion to exalt popular and domestic virtues; expositions of animals and agricultural products were held side-by-side with exhibitions of sculptures and paintings on historical or otherwise educational themes, along with musical performances, prize games, and dances.

Facing page: The temple dedicated to Pythagoras on an artificial island in the lake in the park of the villa.
Following pages: Two interiors of neogothic inspiration.

NEOGOTHIC, NEOCLASSICAL, AND NEOMANNERISM OF THE *FOLLIES* AT VILLA RONCIONI

Antonio di Guelfo added to the Roncioni family's patrimony with the purchase of a Pisan villa in 1468. At the end of the sixteenth century, on the property at Pugnano, his descendants built a "big house" by uniting the old farm houses that sat on the estate at the foot of Monte Pisano. Almost two hundred years later, Francesco Roncioni commissioned Giuseppe Gaetano Nicolai to turn the "big house" into an authentic villa, a project completed in 1779. The result was a traditionally styled structure with a dominating central building and two lateral wings. The interior of the villa, with its profusion of eighteenth- and nineteenth-century decorations, is considerably more modern in tone.

In the central salon, painted architectural illusions include a portico with a false stairway that leads towards the ceiling and a fictitious balustrade where an allegorical representation of *Spring* shines in glory. On the vault over the staircase there is a sumptuous colonnade. These pictorial effects were created by the Neapolitan Pasquale Cioffo in 1781. In other rooms the effects are more neoclassical in style, with joyous Bacchic scenes beyond the airy loggias, fantastic landscapes filtered through transparent curtains, vaporous and complex hangings in the Directoire style in *trompe l'oeil*.

The villa's garden provides the opportunity for an exploration of a number of the main debating points in the realm of artistic philosophy during the first half of the nineteenth century. The garden contains a variety of architectural objects of notably different styles and functional intent. The most impressive of these follies is the neo-Gothic silkworm nursery built in 1831 by Alessandro Gherardesca, an architect from Pisa. It contains the characteristics of an ancient Gothic abbey, with its terracotta statues, spires, pointed pediments, mullioned windows, and pinnacles. The building's ground floor served as a silk mill, while the upper floor was divided into areas dedicated to the cultivation of silk worms. The making of silk was the main activity of the owners. An updated example of Gothic Revival, the silk mill did not share in the era's more theatrical displays of the fantastic, exemplified by the dreamy spires of Horace Walpole's Strawberry Hill in the revived, luxurious perpendicular style. Gherardesca, by contrast, was possessed of moral aspirations and intrigued by the technological innovations introduced in the English architecture of the early Industrial age. In line with the paternalistic organization of the Roncioni establishment, the architect sought to provide the mill's workers with more spacious and light-filled surroundings than was customary. In addition to the silk mill, he built a romantic hermitage in the park, a chapel, and a nymphaeum. The chapel, dating to 1846, recalls the idioms of the local

Detail of the arched entrance to the nymphaeum and the interior of the grotto, faced with a mineral and artificial covering.

Facing page: Vault over the staircase of the villa, painted with illusionistic architectural features.
Following pages: A living room with vaporous neoclassical drapery painted as trompe l'oeil *on the walls.*

Gothic style and makes reference to the precious lacework of Santa Maria della Spina
in Pisa. Gherardesca used fourteenth-century mullioned windows for the apex of the
prospect. For the nymphaeum, free of moral connotation and destined only for
pleasure, Gherardesca worked with a neoclassical approach, unbridling himself in the
interior in an amusing revisitation of the necromantic grotto of the Mannerist style.
The decoration is free of obscure symbolic meanings, but does make use of the familiar
Mannerist repertoire of rustic mosaics, artificial and natural concretions, crystals
and small, shell-shaped fountains in marble. The entrance to the grotto is a simplified
central arch amidst sculptures and neoclassical half-columns carved in homage to the
dreamlike designs of the Prussian architect Karl Friedrich Schinkel, in particular the
Masonic set designs Schinkel conceived for Mozart's *Magic Flute*. At the beginning
of the nineteenth century, the avenues of the romantic park, scattered with Etruscan
archeological ruins, were the scene of the young poet Ugo Foscolo's love for Isabella
Roncioni. His *Ultime Lettere di Jacopo Ortis* (The Last Letters of Jacopo Ortis) are
a testament to his passion.

THE CASTLE OF SAMMEZZANO:
A MOORISH DREAM
IN THE TUSCAN COUNTRYSIDE

A distant view of the castle of Sammezzano does not begin to hint at the wild decorative fantasies that abound within. In the middle of the last century, among the hills of the Valdarno, at the foot of Monte di Vallombrosa, deep within harsh terrain, this bizarre revisitation of Moorish decorative style took life. The villa's gentleman owner, Ferdinando Panciatichi, created a sort of Alhambra amidst his vast property between Rignano sull'Arno and Incisa.

Sammezzano was first the possession of the Altovitis, an aristocratic Florentine family. By decree of Cosimo I it passed to Giovan Jacopo de' Medici, Marchese di Marignano, who subsequently deeded it to Sebastiano Ximenes in the second half of the sixteenth century. Sebastiano, of Portuguese origin, was a senator and lord of Saturnia. His family line, of which he was the progenitor in Tuscany, could also vaunt the prestigous name of Aragon. The main branch of the family came to an end in 1816 with the death of Ferdinando Ximenes d'Aragona, and after a long and tortuous trial, all his possessions and noble titles passed to his nephew Ferdinando, the first born of his sister and her husband Niccolò Panciatichi.

In conceiving his exotic Islamic palace, Ferdinando Panciatichi must certainly have been inspired by a number of popular, mostly English, travelogues and art-tourist guide books that were distributed all over Europe. Two volumes by Owen Jones published in 1842 and 1843 made the splendors of the Alhambra part of the collective Western imagination. The spirited, cosmopolitan circle of English expatriates in Tuscany introduced these volumes and others like them into the sleepy cultural atmosphere of nineteenth-century Florence.

With the exception of the Sala degli Amanti (Lovers' Room), whose ornamental theme is the Age of Chivalry, the interior of the castle is an explosion of Moorish decoration. Diverse techniques and materials compete to give life to a fantastic vision of the palace of the Moorish kings in Granada. Simultaneously opulent and severe, the style of the interior veers from the voluptuous and picturesque mode more common to the era. There is the sumptuously colored stucco of the vaults of the Sala dei Pavoni (Peacocks' Room), its marble-skirted walls covered with ceramic; there is the totally white design of the ballroom; there is the main room, graced with a coffered ceiling and stained-glass windows. More ceramic, tiles, stucco, and stained glass decorate the Sala dei Gigli (Room of Lilies), and the Sala del Giuramento (Oath). The Sala delle Stalattiti (Room of Stalactites) is decorated with a profusion of artificial stalactites and brightly painted columns. The Sala dei Piatti Spagnoli (Room of Spanish Plates) takes its name from the dozens of glazed ceramic plates studded bizarrely into the room's ceiling.

Details of monochromatic decorations in the "Ballroom."

Facing page: The Ballroom decorated with white stucco of Moorish inspiration.

Following pages: Prospect of the castle.

This page: Details of the geometrical polychrome decorations in ceramic that cover the walls and floors of the rooms in the castle.
Facing page: The splendid "Peacock Room" with its luxurious decoration.

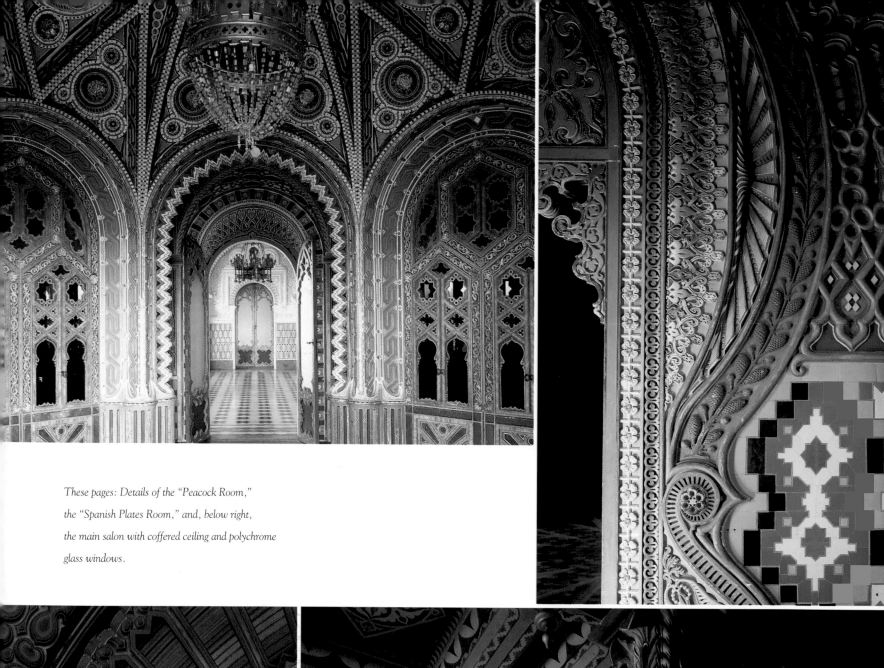

These pages: Details of the "Peacock Room,"
the "Spanish Plates Room," and, below right,
the main salon with coffered ceiling and polychrome
glass windows.

THE ANGLO-AMERICAN COMMUNITY
AT VILLA LA PIETRA

Villa La Pietra came into being around 1460, at the height of the Renaissance. The villa was the work of Francesco Sassetti, who was Lorenzo de' Medici's banker and Ghirlandaio's patron for his work on the frescoes in the chapel of the Santa Trinità in Florence. The baroque facade of the villa, attributed to Carlo Fontana, and the three levels of the garden are grafted together with a series of balustrades and stairways. Much of the work on this part of the villa dates back to the second half of the seventeenth century when the Capponi family were the owners. In the nineteenth century the Prussian Ambassador resided at La Pietra, and the formal garden underwent a romantic transformation. The real golden period of the villa began in the first years of the twentieth century when it was bought by Sir Harold Acton. A great deal of restoration work was performed and the garden was returned to its original form—a splendid continuation of clearings ornamented by eighteenth-century Venetian statues, the works of Bonazza and Orazio Marinali. There are box hedges and avenues covered with banksia roses between walls of holm oaks and cypress trees. At the end of the garden there is a bright shining Corinthian colonnade. Inside there is an eclectic collection of paintings, sculpture, and furniture from various periods, particularly the Renaissance.

Under Acton, La Pietra became a brilliant cultural and cosmopolitan center. The sophisticated, intellectual, Italianized Anglo-American universe of which it was such an important part is evoked in the pages of Edith Wharton and Henry James. This was the elegant age of Bernard Berenson and Lady Sybil Cuffe Cutting at Villa Medici, of Vernon Lee and Cecil Pinsent, of the three eccentric Sitwells at Castle Montegufoni. Acton himself was a fascinating individual, a highly regarded scholar and author of, among other works, *The Last Medici* and an extraordinary autobiography, *Memoirs of an Aesthete*. He bequeathed the villa and the garden to New York University.

One of the eighteenth-century statues that decorate the garden of Villa La Pietra.

Facing page: The stairway to the terrace on the facade of the villa.

This page: Glimpses of the garden at Villa La Pietra, decorated with statues and box hedges.

Facing page: Another glimpse of the late-nineteenth-century garden, outlined with a formal plan of seventeenth- and eighteenth-century inspiration.

Villa interior, splendid furniture, and paintings

of various periods blend harmoniously in a universal

collection that reverberates with the passion of its last

proprietor, Sir Harold Acton.

166

ECHOES OF THE *BELLE EPOQUE*
AT THE BATHS OF MONTECATINI

Detail of decoration in ceramic by Galileo Chini.

The waters of Montecatini, almost certainly known to the ancients, are recorded from the fourteenth century on. By the first years of the sixteenth century a number of baths had been built upon orders of the Florentine Signoria. There are eight salt-sulphate-alcaline springs active in Montecatini today. In 1583 the territory and the springs entered into the patrimony of the Medici, already passionate admirers of the Baths in Lucca and San Casciano. The Medicis left the baths untouched, and it was only in 1740 that Francesco II of Lorraine, grand duke of Tuscany, ordered some restoration work to be done. It was Leopoldo I, at the end of the eighteenth century, who began to use the thermal waters under the advisement of a group of men inspired by the Enlightenment, among them Giovanni Targioni Tozzetti and Abbott Guido Grandi. Leopoldo employed the services of the architect Gaspare Paoletti who reclaimed the flat land at the foot of the Montecatini hill and built the important Baths of Leopoldino and the Tettuccio. In 1784 the Lorraine grand duke donated the baths to the Benedictines of the Badia in Florence, and they built the Bagno del Rinfresco, the first hotel Locanda Maggiore, and a hospital known as *la caserma dei poveri* (the barracks of the poor). The Napoleonic confiscations in 1815 secularized the baths, and with the Restoration they were conceded to three noblemen from Pescia, who improved the equipment.

Montecatini began to attract international attention in the mid-nineteenth century; by the end of the century its renown had grown still greater, thanks to the rationalization of the water basin made by Pietro Grocco. In 1905 there was a ferment of construction, of hotels and other buildings. The private springs were united and the Società delle Terme was founded. The Society carried out a significant series of improvements, transformed Montecatini by 1927 into one of the most popular thermal baths in Europe. The *Belle Epoque* brought to the area Balkan monarchs, Russian princes, and serene highnesses from Central Europe. Notables such as Giuseppe Verdi and Nellie Melba were often seen strolling down the elegant walks upon which opened the main bathing establishments, from the neoclassical Leopoldine Baths, built in 1775 and reconfigured in this century, to the Excelsior, in Liberty style, built in 1927. At the end of the avenue the Terme Tettuccio rises. It is a monumental marble edifice with floral elements in iron and stained glass, marble floors, mosaics and frescoes by Galileo Chini, formal parks, and a circular basin around which rise the entire architectural grid. It was a setting destined for a community of elite tourists that has largely disappeared today. The experience of the Baths in their heyday is relived in the film *Oci Ciornie* (Dark Eyes) by the Soviet director Nikita Mikhalkov, with the extraordinary Marcello Mastroianni as the lead. Mastroianni, of course, also played the principal character in Fellini's famed *8-1/2*, much of which was shot in the luxurious, contemporary setting of the Liberty-style baths of Berzieri at Salsomaggiore.

Facing page: Detail from the Liberty fountain, with inserts of colored glass that decorates the central oval basin of the Terme Tettuccio at Montecatini.

Cupola decorated with Art Nouveau frescos,

testifying to the great decorative richness that abounds

in the thermal building.

Liberty glass and stucco decorate the thermal buildings,
and accentuate the exclusive character of the
sophisticated international clientele that made the
fortune of Montecatini.

REGINA

REGINA

Above and facing page: The sequence of ceramic panels that decorate the wall behind the bar, painted by Galileo Chini.

Following pages: Details of a Liberty cantilever roof in iron and colored glass, and of the curved colonnade that enclosed the central basin in the thermal buildings of Tettuccio.

STUDIOS AND LABORATORIES
OF ART
AND ARTISTIC CRAFTSMANSHIP

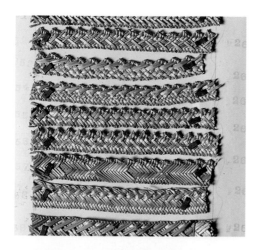

*Samples of Florentine straw products and some
terracotta vases from Impruneta.*

*Facing page: The antique cupboards
of the perfumery/pharmacy of Santa Maria Novella.*

The jewel box of marvels that is the famous Studiolo of Francesco I at Palazzo Vecchio
still reverberates with the Medici passion for collecting. It contains the once virturally
inaccessible magnificence of the grand ducal workshops. Porcelain, gold and silver
work, majolica, laboratories of arrases and bronze, the marvelous, multicolored works
in pietra dura, sumptuous textile work, perfume workshops (the famous Santa Maria
Novella, dating back to the fourteenth century, is still active), all were part of the
opulent mosaic of the Tuscan court. Paintings from the late-sixteenth-century artists
of the school of Vasari were displayed, as a great privilege, in this room. Celebrating
human achievement, they are direct testimony to the productive, innovative spirit
of their age. The Medici's gold workshop is depicted, with Cellini intent on refining the
grand-ducal crown. We can see the blacksmiths in the forge of Vulcan, the wool
workers at their trade. One of the prides of Tuscany, the region's wool industry to this
day produces original fabrics such as the *rustico Casentino*. The women spinning and
embroidering as painted in the Sala di Penelope represent a history of the
craftsmanship that is still very much alive across the entire region. A visit to the
Florentine and other Tuscan craftsmen's workshops reveals how the region has been
able to preserve its many arts. Many young people are employed and the atmosphere
of vitality and energy leads to results of a very high quality.

Tuscany, and Florence in particular, still reveals much that is beautiful and unexpected
from the border land between art and craftsmanship. Although many crafts activities
have had to leave the center of the city for various reasons and transfer to the
immediate environs, one need only wander around the narrow streets of Santo Spirito
or in San Frediano. There are glass makers and glass engravers, bronze makers,
lacquerers, sculptors in wood, inlayers of ivory, goldsmiths, all working with infinite
skill and patience. Nearly forgotten techniques, for example, are employed to restore
the exquisite furniture of Maggiolini. New techniques are constantly being developed.
A trip to the region's studios and laboratories enables one to revisit the ancient skill
that the craftsman brings to his art and that art brings to the craftsman.

There is an ongoing exchange of technical ability and aesthetic creativity between expert technicians and artists of genius. Impruneta, for example, a large village not far from Florence, has been noted for centuries for its terracotta ovens and brick kilns. They are the same workshops that served Filippo Brunelleschi for the wonderful cupola of Santa Maria del Fiore in Florence.

Many of the great terracotta vases used for the perfumed lemon plants that punctuate the box-hedge parterre design of the typical Tuscan garden are products of the village. Vases in the form of shells decorated Mannerist-style with masks and scrolls, Della Robbia or neoclassical garlands, coats of arms and monograms—all come from Impruneta, as do oil jars and a variety of construction details that form part of the local architectural language. The famous Florentine straw was another Tuscan specialty, particularly in the last century with the fashion for broad-brimmed hats spurred by the romantic *Pamela* portraits of Winterhalter and the exquisite beauties of Renoir.

Below: Ancient and modern examples of Florentine straw.
Facing page: The laboratory of a sculptor and wood carver.

THE ANCIENT ART OF INLAY

Details of inlay of semi-precious stones.

Above: A figurative motif.

Below: The coat of arms of the city of Florence.

Facing page: Detail of a decorative panel in inlay
of semi-precious stones preserved in the Opificio delle
Pietre Dure in Florence.

The Florentine Opificio delle Pietre Dure, at one time in the Uffizi, was created by Ferdinando I de' Medici at the end of the sixteenth century to train and discipline specialized craftsmen in the working of pietra dura and precious stones. Before Ferdinando, the grand duke Cosimo too had encouraged this art, and it was already on its way to becoming an authentic Florentine speciality. The institutionalization of the Opificio was contemporaneous with the construction of the Cappella dei Principi, intended to be a signal work of Florentine decoration, with the typical marble inlay of the Tuscan masters.

Annexed to the Opificio is the Museo delle Pietre Dure. Restoration work is also done here. The museum holds a rich collection of objects in pietra dura and in scagliola, of mosaic, of paintings on stone, and of cameos. The Medici collection of marble materials used in the laboratory of the Opificio is very important, not least for its unrivaled collection of works in scagliola. Scagliola—a gypsum-and-glue-based imitation of ornamental stone—came into being at the beginning of the sixteenth century and had fallen into disuse by the end of the nineteenth century. The most famed practitioner of the art of scagliola was Henry Hugford, born in Florence of English parents in 1695. In the 1930s, Italian artists attempted to revive of its use, largely in an effort to preserve a unique national tradition. Scagliola, speckled with colored stone and earth to resemble mosaic, is filled, with mallet and scalpel, into the deeply sculpted areas in a slab of marble to be used as a table top or a piece of furniture. The first step is to trace the chosen design onto the stone surface and then etch it in. After about two weeks, when the compound of marble fragments has solidified, one can proceed to the smoothing of the surface with water and pumice, and then, as the final step, engrave the smaller and most essential details. In the works of scagliola at the museum, we can see fantastic landscapes, panoplies of armies and compositions of musical and scientific instruments, astrological and zodiacal themes still being reproduced in exactly the same way as they were in the baroque age over two hundred years ago.

Above: Preparation of a decorative border in scagliola.

Below: Detail of a panel depicting Fame, from a design
by Bernardino Poccetti, preserved at the Opificio delle
Pietre Dure.

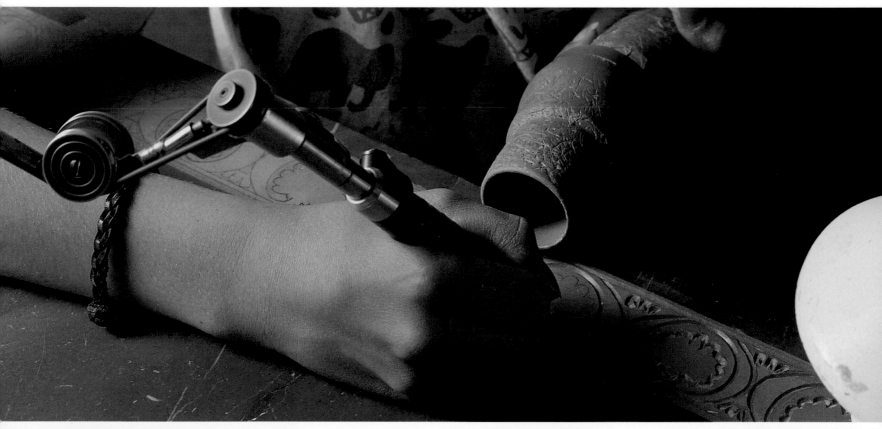

FLORENTINE SILK
FOR THE ARISTOCRACY

Silk was introduced into Italy around 1100, probably by Catholic missionaries to China, or, as a charming legend has it, by an Oriental princess who came as a bride to Europe, and brought the silk grub with her. By the fourteenth century Florence was already a leading trade center, making the city particularly appropriate for the nurturing of a silk industry. Silk was the origin of the fortunes of many of the most ancient patrician Florentine families, like the Rucellai, who discovered the crimson-colored silk that made them immensely wealthy. In the mid-seventeenth century a number of Florentine families, among them the Guicciardini, the Della Gherardesca, the Pucci, the Corsini, the Bartolozzi, and the Agresti, decided to set up a common laboratory and factory that would continue to produce each family's original designs while taking advantage of economies of scale. The headquarters were set up in via de' Tessitori. The fabrics soon attracted the attention of an eager public and the Antico Setificio Fiorentino became recognized around Europe for the quality of its products. In 1786 the offices were transferred to their present location at 4 via Bartolini, and the factory continued to produce high-quality silks throughout the nineteenth century and into the twentieth.

After World War II, Marchese Emilio Pucci di Barsento, famous personality of the fashion world, became a majority shareholder in the factory and launched it into the international marketplace. In 1987, his son Alessandro took over the business. He has focused on the restoration of antique looms and continued to uphold the centuries-old tradition of quality fabrics. Production today is geared to an exclusive clientele, including a number of royal houses of Europe, and museums and public institutions such as the Quirinale, the Senate, and Palazzo Madama. Current production lines include a large range of damasks in Renaissance silk, brocatelle in silk and linen of various eras, and eighteenth-century lampas rigorously woven by hand on eighteenth-century looms. The sarsanet, a kind of Renaissance silk taffeta, has a magical quality, luminous and shining. It is the fabric that clothes many of the splendid Renaissance ladies painted by Masolino, Masaccio, and Piero della Francesca, as well as those in the Mannerist portraits of Pontormo and Bronzino. Still produced in three traditional weights—light, single thread, and double—the fabric is now used for furnishings. The Silk Factory also produces typical Florentine fabrics with specially spun material made to order, such as woven silk, turkey twill, the famous floss silk, and the grosgrain of pure silk. The dyeing is still done by hand, and the careful weaving process creates a fabric that is inimitable in its texture, color, and strength.

Details of the dress worn by Lucrezia Panciatichi, in the painting by Agnolo Bronzino, preserved in the Galleria degli Uffizi in Florence.

Facing page: Cupboard containing ribbons and grosgrain in the office of the Antico Setificio Fiorentino. Following pages: The laboratory where the fabrics are woven on antique looms.

THE WHITE GOLD OF THE APUAN ALPS

Two sculptures in the studio of Botero at Pietrasanta.

Facing page: A marble quarry in the Apuan Alps.

The area between Versilia and the Apuan Alps has been famous since Roman times for its marble quarries. This area, extending as far as the great mountain landscape of Campanagrina, includes the village of Pietrasanta, the towns of Querceta, Avenza, Serravezza, Stazzema, and the cities of Massa and Carrara. The marble quarrying industry in the region dates back two thousand years and is regulated by laws some of which are unchanged since 1751, and will not be revised definitively until 2004. The Apuans in the Carrara area, and especially the valley of the Carrione, are rich in marble deposits, and constitute one of the world's major centers of production and commerce in the stone. The marble is divided into numerous varieties according to color and structure, among which the most important is the rare *statuario*, used almost exclusively for sculpture. The Apuans also produce the *bianco chiaro ordinario* (ordinary clear white), the *bianco porcellana* (porcelain white), various shades of *bardiglio*, from *Grigio* to *turchinaccio* (grey to turquoise), the yellowish *paonazzo*, the *fior di pesco* (peach flower), the greenish *Cipollino Apuano*, the *Arabescato* of the Upper Versilia area, the predominantly orange *breccia medicea*, and the variegated *breccia violetta*. There are more than a thousand quarries, counting those still being mined and those that have been abandoned. The quarries open out on the valley slopes to an altitude of three thousand feet. While the extraction techniques have, of course, changed greatly over the centuries, the use of dynamite is limited. Recently, a debate sparked by ecologists concerned with the progressive destruction of the Apuan mountains has become even more heated. What has changed least over time is the character and lives of the miners themselves. They are the custodians of an ancestral knowledge. Many families have been in the business for centuries and their secret skills and particular methods are passed down from father to son. The miner is always attuned to any signs of danger given off by the mountain, with which he has a visceral, even deeply personal relationship. Much as they did hundreds of years ago, men continue to challenge the mountains in the quest for rocks of calcium carbonate—pure marble, "white gold" under the open sky.

The studio at Pietrasanta, in the province of Lucca, where Botero works some months of the year.

That marble destined for statuary is worked in laboratories or workshops using modern equipment and specialized labor that comes from the local Scuola del Marmo (Marble School), next door to the Accademia delle Belle Arti. The 25,000 square meters of marble used for the grandiose Arc de la Défense in Paris, the stone facings of much postmodern American architecture, the marble facades that grace so many contemporary Asian skyscrapers, all come from here. From Michelangelo to Canova, from Henry Moore to Botero—who spends many months a year near Pietrasanta in order to prepare his sculptures—artists through the ages have measured themselves against this extraordinary and inimitable material.

A laboratory in Carrara, for the production of marble

for artists.